A GIFT TO IMAGINE

THE BLISS OF BEING G-PA

SCOTT LUDWIG

A GIFT TO IMAGINE
THE BLISS OF BEING G-PA

iUniverse books may be ordered through booksellers or by contacting:

iUniverse
1663 Liberty Drive
Bloomington, IN 47403
www.iuniverse.com
1-800-Authors (1-800-288-4677)

Because of the dynamic nature of the Internet, any web addresses or links contained in this book may have changed since publication and may no longer be valid. The views expressed in this work are solely those of the author and do not necessarily reflect the views of the publisher, and the publisher hereby disclaims any responsibility for them.

Any people depicted in stock imagery provided by Thinkstock are models, and such images are being used for illustrative purposes only. Certain stock imagery © Thinkstock.

ISBN: 978-1-4917-7477-9 (sc)
ISBN: 978-1-4917-7478-6 (e)

Print information available on the last page.

iUniverse rev. date: 08/21/2015

Dedication

To Krischan,

Who has—and is—a gift to imagine.

And to grandparents everywhere:

They'll get this book.

Contents

Foreword

I've been writing about my grandson Krischan since the day he was born. Believe me: It is—and continues to be---a labor of love.

People have told me they enjoy reading my stories and what a joy it must be to have Krischan in my life. Some have even told me I ought to write a book about our adventures together.

Well, I took that advice. You may have noticed, seeing as you're holding it in your hands at this very moment. I'd like to tell you I wrote it for you, Dear Reader, but that wouldn't be the truth.

I wrote it for Krischan. One day I want him to be able to look back on his childhood years and remember it was his G-Pa who told him to always say please and thank you and to look both ways before crossing the street. I want him to remember the two of us watching his first movie at the 'thee-tee-er' and crossing the finish line together in his first road race. I want him to reminisce about hunting zombies in the woods behind my house, eating 'spicy candy' until our stomachs ached and watching cartoons over and over again until we both knew what the characters would say next… every single time.

The joys of being a grandfather have been experienced and understood for many, many years. See for yourself in these well-documented quotes:

One of the most powerful handclasps is that of a new grandson around the finger of a grandfather.

There is no grandfather who does not adore his grandson.

There are also a few other quotes I came across that provide even more insight into the relationship:

A grandparent is old on the outside but young on the inside.

Grandparents are there to help the child get into mischief they haven't thought of yet.

And my personal favorite and one that hits the nail directly on the head:

My grandson believes I'm the oldest person in the world. After a couple of hours with him, I believe it too.

One other thing you should know: I also wrote this book so that one day when Krischan becomes an astronaut, finds a cure for cancer or becomes the 55th President of the United States he can remember the day when he was five years old and pointed to a picture in a book he was looking at and told me in the most solemn tone you'll ever hear from someone his age:

'That's bamboon, G-Pa. You know, what a panda eats.'

K-Man,

I hope this book will warm your heart, put a smile on your face and serve as a constant reminder that I will always be with you.

I wrote this book before you started first grade. I want you to remember all of the things I taught you before you went off to school and began your formal education.

More importantly, I want you to remember you taught me a thing or two as well.

We make a great team.

Love,

G-Pa

Central Cast of Characters

Krischan – The Grandson (Krischan is the Greek spelling of 'Christian')

Yia-Yia (Cindy) – The Grandmother (Yia-Yia is Greek for 'Grandmother')

G-Pa (Scott) – The Grandfather (G-Pa is a cool and catchy nickname in any language)

Justin – Krischan's Father

Josh – Krischan's Uncle and Justin's Brother

Maui, Molly, Millie, Moe and Morgan – The Cats

Full Circle - Part One

I just came back from running 100 miles in the Black Hills of South Dakota. My body was beaten to a pulp and my mind wasn't in particularly great shape either. My wife Cindy picked me up at the Atlanta airport and once I got in the car (not as easy as it sounds, considering the pain I was in) she asked me the usual questions she always did when I returned from running one of my longer races. Then I asked her what was new with her and she told me that one of the cats had thrown up, that she had gone shopping with her best friend while I was away and that we were having soup for dinner. Pretty standard fare, with one tiny last-second addition: 'Oh, and you're going to be a grandfather.' If nothing else the news made the physical pain I was in take a back seat to the apprehension I was suddenly feeling about that last little bit of news… taking into account that up until that precise moment in time becoming a grandfather wasn't anything within the realms of my wildest imagination.

On March 24, 2009—211 days after Cindy told me I was going to become a grandfather—I met Krischan for the very first time. He was only a couple of hours old and wearing a light blue knit cap on his head and a white hospital bracelet on his left wrist, his right thumb tucked securely in his mouth. The rest of his tiny body was snuggly wrapped in a blanket and as much as I wanted to pick him up and hold him I didn't want to risk waking him from his deep, peaceful sleep. I put myself in his booties for a second and decided I wouldn't want to be disturbed after a nine-month journey like he had just been on, so I just let him sleep. The fact we didn't make eye contact on the day he was born—that wouldn't happen until several days later—didn't stand in the way of me realizing the second I laid eyes on Krischan that I loved that little boy with all my heart.

I thought back to the day my first son Justin—Krischan's father—was born and how my dad wept as he held his grandson in his arms for the first

1

time, minutes after he was officially blessed with the title of 'grandfather.' I wondered that day—and I remember it well even though it had occurred almost 27 years earlier—how I would feel when the same thing happened to me: On the day I would become a grandfather.

The easiest way to explain it is by saying simply:

My life had come full circle.

It was now my turn.

My turn to discover the magic, the wonder and the joy of being a grandfather.

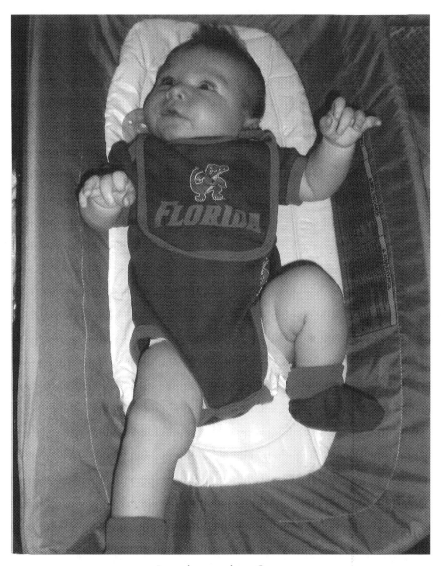

I was born to be a Gator

Children make you want to start life over.
-Muhammad Ali

Full Circle - Part Two

June 2012

One hot summer afternoon in the early 1980's I was staying at my parents' home in Virginia Beach and invited my dad to run three miles. Keep in mind that I had been running for a few years and was in my early 20's while my dad was a virtual novice to running and in his early 50's. Dad ran the entire three miles—and I was with him every step of the way, my shins screaming for mercy due to the pain from the running-with-the-parking-brake-on motion I was subjecting my legs to in order to accommodate my dad's eleven-minute-mile pace.

On a recent hot summer afternoon during my second run of the day I found my shins—along with a few other parts of my body screaming for mercy due to the is-this-the-best-I-can-do motion I was subjecting them to in order to accommodate MY eleven-minute-mile pace.

There's a phrase for what transpired: Coming full circle. Some may refer to it as karma. Or perhaps kismet.

Or, as my good friend of mine says whenever we find ourselves not living up to what our former selves (and by 'selves' I mean 'bodies') were able to do:

It's come to this.

Flash forward to the afternoon of Sunday, June 10, 2012. I was walking out the front door with my grandson Krischan (just over three years old) when he looked at me and said 'I want to run like you, G-Pa.' Three things immediately came to mind: (1) That sentence was music to my ears; (2) I'm pretty sure my heart just melted; and (3) If Krischan wants to run then gosh darn he was going to.

I dropped everything and instructed Krischan to run to the bush on the far side of the front yard and back again. Instead he took off and ran around the circular stone flowerbed in the front yard. Not only did Krischan instinctively run the course in a counter-clockwise direction (as a track runner would do), he also displayed an almost flawless running motion (a virtually still head, a forceful and driving arm swing and an even pace) that his G-Pa has NEVER displayed. Krischan proceeded to run exactly... four... laps. Once he finished he walked over to tell me he was tired... and immediately returned to the flowerbed and ran another four laps, a virtual carbon copy of his first four laps. He walked back over to me and said yet again that he was tired, and this time I knew it to be true, as he was beginning to perspire and breathing a bit heavier than normal.

I told Krischan how proud I was of him and that I would take him to a real track the following weekend. I asked him where he learned to run so well and... well, he just giggled as only three-year-olds-who-know-how-to-melt-your-heart can do.

Later that afternoon I measured the circular path Krischan had run around the flowerbed. Exactly 75 feet. In other words Krischan had *(instinctively, perhaps?)* run exactly 100 yards.

Call it karma. Call it kismet. Call it what you will.

But know this: Krischan had shown me my life had come full circle.

And I was *loving* it!

Postscript: Six days later I took Krischan to the rubberized 400-meter track at Riley Field in Peachtree City, Georgia. Immediately upon reaching the track Krischan, without instruction or prodding, took off running in a counter-clockwise direction with the same still head, arm swing and even pace he demonstrated around the flowerbed. He ran an entire lap—*four hundred meters* before stopping to catch his breath for a few seconds before heading out for another lap.

It appears I may need to hold on to that eleven-minute-pace a little while longer.

You know, so I can keep up with my grandson.

I took my first bath where the dirty dishes go

You can learn many things from children. How much patience you have, for instance.
-Franklin P. Jones

Couch Potatoes

March 2013

As today was a pretty eventful day for a non-eventful day, a few highlights from yesterday:

Cindy and her business partner Tracy celebrated the one-year anniversary of their store and the timing couldn't have been better; they met with their accountant earlier in the week and learned they made a solid profit in their first 10 months. They plan to re-invest their profit into a second store with intentions of a grand opening this summer. Knowing them like I do, it will most certainly happen. My two sons, Krischan and I dropped by for the anniversary and took them a sheet cake with their store logo decorating the top of it.

After the four of us had lunch (Krischan had mac-n-cheese and a fruit cup along with two bites of shrimp out of my po-boy sandwich. Why am I telling you this? Patience.). Justin and Josh went back to Justin's house to lift weights so I took Krischan home with me. Highlights of the drive home:

Krischan: Are we going to your house? I like your house. It's shaped like a rectangle. I like rectangles.

Me: What do you want to do today?

Krischan: I want to watch (*The*) *Lorax* with you. He talks to the trees.
Me: I can't believe you asked me that. Do you know that exactly one year ago today I took you to see *The Lorax*. It was the first time you went to a movie theater.

Krischan: Let's go to a movie theater today.

Me: I thought you wanted to see *The Lorax*.
Krischan: Do you have it?

Me: No, but you do; I gave you a copy for Christmas.

Krischan: It's in my room. In Texas. Let's play basketball instead.

(We stopped at a store on the way home. I let him pick out a few toy dinosaurs as he is fascinated with them, and I felt a little guilty because I couldn't remember where I put his *Dinosaur Train* play set. Krischan's dad had the same fascination—initially with sharks, then Michael Jordan, then heavy metal and then horror movies—that began about the time he was Krischan's age.)

Krischan: I want that one; it's a T Rex. And this Stegosaurus. And this one; it's a Triceratops. And the Allosaurus. And the Brachiosaurus. And this (an)other T Rex. And this dinosaur bird (After Krischan, as I would later discover after doing a little research on the internet, had correctly identified those first six dinosaurs I was a bit surprised he didn't know the Pterodactyl. Know this: He does now.).

We ended up spending the rest of the day doing the thing he likes to do most: Following his G-Pa wherever and whenever he goes. So all in all, yesterday was a very good day, and ended with Krischan sleeping next to his 'best friend in the whole wide world: G-Pa.'

Which leads me to today.

My day started at 1:45 a.m. I was awakened by Krischan's rather loud 'slurping.' It sounded as if he was sipping a drink through a straw. I found it odd because I didn't remember Krischan taking a drink to bed with him or waking up to ask me to get him one. After 30 seconds or so Krischan, who had his back to me up until this time rolled over and said four little words that caused my hair to stand on end:

9

G-Pa, I threw up.

Man, did he ever! There was a perfect circle two-feet-in-diameter consisting of dark green vomit (and two hardly-chewed pieces of shrimp) a mere foot or so away from me, and in between the vomit and I was my grandson who was literally bathed in dark green paint from the waist up.

But it didn't end there. The comforter, the blanket, the sheets and the pillow were now all perfectly color-coordinated with Krischan's pajama top. I called Cindy, who was sleeping in the bedroom down the hall and told her I needed her help. Once she arrived her 'help' basically consisted of keeping her gag reflex in check and reminding me 'this is your end; I handle the other end' (which made me wonder why I had been on wiping duty thus far into Krischan's visit). It took almost 90 minutes to get everything cleaned up before we were able to lie back down and try to go back to sleep, about which time Krischan decided he was hungry.

Eventually I believe we both got back to sleep around 3:45; I had the alarm set for 4:30 as I was running with a friend at 5:40. Cindy climbed in bed with Krischan when I left for my run so she could keep her eyes on him.

After the events of earlier that morning, the frigid morning air (mid-30's and a moderate wind) actually felt refreshing. I returned from my run at 8:15, only to find Krischan and Cindy still asleep/keeping her eyes on him (*your call*).

When Krischan woke up he was still vomiting, but it was no longer dark green; it was now clear. Apparently there was nothing left in his stomach. To make matters worse, he wasn't hungry, he wasn't thirsty and he now had diarrhea just to, you know, keep things interesting.

Cindy and I were volunteering after that morning's church service so we were fortunate our younger son Josh was staying with us; he could keep his eyes on Krischan while we were gone. Before we left, however, we had to break the bad news to Krischan: he would not be going to church with us (and he *loves* going to church).

The instant Cindy told him he would need to stay home he reacted exactly as you expected he would: his eyes welled up with tears. I felt like the evil villain in a 1960's John Wayne cowboy movie but then I thought that the evil villain wouldn't know the first thing about what it felt like to be viewed as an evil villain so just never mind with this analogy and move on to the next paragraph.

Krischan was missed at church, as evidenced by the handful of candy we were given by some members of the congregation who were hoping they would get to see him. After the service Cindy and I met Tracy and her husband for lunch at the new Mexican restaurant in town. During lunch they wondered why Krischan wasn't with us, so Cindy told them about him being sick and this morning's vomit extravaganza and how difficult it was to clean everything up, all the time never once bothering to say that I was the one responsible for cleaning everything up seeing as she was too busy gagging and holding her breath and all. Being the good husband I can be when I want to be, I didn't say a word.

After lunch we all visited the tentative site for Cindy's second store that she hopes to open this summer. Seeing as today was the first day of the second year their original store opened, it was sort of a karma/kismet/poetic/cosmic *(I'm not sure what word I'm looking for, but I'm pretty sure it's one of these)* moment.

When Cindy and I got home Krischan was asleep on the couch. It was 3:00 p.m. He had originally got on the couch at 9:00 a.m., getting up only to use the bathroom. My precious little guy was indeed sick; a victim, apparently of the dreaded stomach flu. Cindy, Josh and I spent the rest of the day with him taking turns performing couch potato duty. No one seemed to mind, especially after last night's sequence of events. (Whom am I kidding? Cindy got twice as much sleep as I did, Josh three times as much and between the two of them Cindy contributed significantly more help to Operation Cleanup than Josh—and you already know what that amounted to.)

After a 9:00 p.m. trip to the grocery store to get Krischan some medicine, I was ready for bed. Cindy mentioned she could still smell the lingering odor of vomit in the house. I told her I didn't notice the smell and when she asked how I could possibly NOT I reminded her I've worked in warehouses for 34 years and during that time I've trained myself to mentally NOT smell anything unless I did so intentionally, a talent that has served me well in a variety of situations over the years. (Two sons, one grandson and five cats, all with 'their own special smells.')

Just before getting into bed, however, my talent failed me. I caught a whiff of an odor that caused me to run to the bathroom and spritz a dose of cologne under my nose, a trick I used in college to counter bad odors--like roommates who bathed only on Friday nights. As it always did, the trick worked like a charm.

I hate to leave you in suspense, but I made a promise to Cindy I would never reveal the source of the odor.

So keeping that promise, I can't tell you what Cindy had for lunch earlier in the day and what it did to her digestive system. After all, I promised.

Loving my first ride in a stroller

Children make your life important.
-Erma Bombeck

Best Friends

March 2013

Today was a vacation day for me. I spent it with my best friend in the whole wide world.

We started the day by driving out to see the gorgeous countryside of Senoia, Georgia. After a quick stop at Crook's Grocery to buy a sack of apples and a bag of carrots, we stopped by the residence of my friend Valerie where I introduced my best friend to Val's dozen or so chickens. After that, a stop along the side of the road to feed the apples and carrots to two of the friendliest horses you'd ever want to meet. The cows (and calves) on the other side of the road, however weren't quite as friendly. Our presumption is they didn't have a lot of experience with humans stopping by to say hello.

We stopped by an old dilapidated house in the woods that was surrounded by the yellow caution tape you would expect to find around a house in that condition. My friend jokingly asked if any zombies lived inside; an odd question seeing as how Senoia lends itself to most of the sights seen in the television series *The Walking Dead*. We then went to the empty town of Haralson; again, the locale for many of the sequences on the same show. Our grand tour wouldn't be complete without a final stop in downtown Senoia, or as it is known on the show, 'Woodbury.'

Our travels then took us to Fayetteville, where we had a late lunch and took in a movie. While we were in the theater, the blustery 64-degree day had turned into a windy, rainy afternoon. We returned to my house afterwards to reflect on what a wonderful day it had been. Never underestimate the value of good conversation with a good friend; especially a *best* friend. We looked at the photographs I had taken throughout the day, glad that we had a history of our day together to reflect back on in the years ahead.

I don't get to see my best friend nearly as often as I would like. It's times like these that make me appreciate what time I have with those who mean the most to me.

Believe me: I'm not trying to preach. I'm just reminding myself how lucky I am to have such a terrific best friend in the whole wide world. I feel certain he knows how much he means to me.

Today was a vacation day for me. It was just what I needed.

Thank you, Krischan. G-Pa loves you.

My first bad hair day

A three-year old child is a being who gets as
much fun out of a $56 set of swings
as it does out of finding a small green worm.
-Bill Vaughan

Hope for the Future

March 2013

Is it just me or is there a total lack of creativity in the world of advertising? Granted, there is the rare television commercial that captures your attention; the early days of the E*TRADE baby and the heart-warming Budweiser Clydesdale commercials, for example. However, radio commercials are a different story altogether: The clever, original radio commercial does not exist. While I'm on this subject, let me add that in my humble opinion any radio commercial that includes the sound of a car horn and/or sirens should be illegal. Have you ever been driving along listening to the radio and suddenly feeling like you're in imminent danger when you hear a blaring horn or siren? Then, after looking around desperately in every possible direction realizing you've essentially been 'punked' by a radio commercial? I thought so. I have as well. Way too often, I might add. I swear one of these days I'll be found slumped over my steering wheel, the victim of a commercially induced heart attack.

What I'm leading up to is this: Today's lack of creativity frightens me. What happened to good old-fashioned American ingenuity? Want another example? Check out an ad for your local movie theater and see how many of the movies are remakes or sequels, or in some cases both.

But there is hope. I spent yesterday with my grandson and let me be the first to tell you: Creativity is not dead. Not by a long shot.

Krischan and I went to my warehouse around lunchtime because I had to catch up on a few things at work... and because Krischan wanted to go to 'G-Pa's workhouse,' as he calls it. After that we headed to the local track because, you know, he 'wanted to run with G-Pa.' We ran a lap around the 400-meter track and were getting ready to run another lap when Krischan discovered the large mat used for pole-vaulting. Once he understood what it was used for, he was intrigued at jumping on it, again and again and again. I was afraid he would spend the afternoon jumping on the mat until he discovered the hurdles. Krischan asked what they were used for and when I told him, he admitted he was too short to jump over them… and preceded to crawl through each and every one of them to illustrate 'he could do it,' which he did again and again and again. I was afraid we would spend the remainder of the afternoon at the hurdles until he discovered… the dried-up mud pit.

Alongside the track was a small patch of dried mud not more than four square feet in size. Krischan discovered it, grabbed a pair of rocks and immediately started throwing them at 'the alligator,' a small clump of dried mud that in all honestly actually did closely resemble an alligator. Before long a small girl—maybe six years old asked if she could play. It struck me funny that she asked if she could play, as if Krischan's imaginary game had rules or was even known among children their age. Krischan said yes and stood up to help her look for some rocks. Once she had the apparently required two rocks she joined in the aerial assault on the reptile. After a few minutes the little girl said her name was Sofia, to which Krischan replied 'Sofia is a princess' (from the cartoon *Sofia the First*) and then 'my name is Krischan.' They played smash-the-gator for a few minutes when Krischan began placing clumps of dried mud in various sizes and referring to them as big and little 'angry birds,' which they had to destroy. Each time Sofia's rock would strike an angry bird, Krischan would raise both of his hands in the air and proclaim 'Oooh, you GOT one!' Then Krischan found a really large clump of mud that they had dislodged from the ground with their many throws. Out of the blue he asked me if beavers had whiskers. When I replied that they did, Krischan placed the large clump in the middle of their 'arena' and said it was a 'giant monster beaver with whiskers' (it had two small white pieces of dead grass sticking out of it that closely resembled the whiskers of a rodent).

Once the business at hand was resolved, Krischan stood up and out of left field said 'let's run.' (He was talking to Sofia, not me.) They proceeded to run a lap around the track while darting in and out of the middle school track team, then caught their breath and resumed their game of Smash the Evil Mud Beasts. The small patch of dried mud was Krischan's playground… his canvas… *his world*. As Sofia's mother said to me at one point: 'Who needs computers?'

Krischan has got quite the imagination. Creativity is not dead: there is hope for the future after all.

Something tells me this kid is going to be just fine.

I've always loved playgrounds; everything about them!

Grandchildren are the dots that connect the
lines from generation to generation.
-Lois Wyse

Never Could Say Goodbye

March 2013

As a child of a father in the United States Navy, I was accustomed to moving every three years when my dad was reassigned to another tour of duty. You would think that after a childhood of bidding farewell to friends, neighbors and teachers again and again I would be fairly comfortable saying goodbye.

If that's what you thought, you couldn't be further from the truth. I suck at goodbyes.

There's a saying about enjoying every moment with someone because it just might be the last time you ever have to spend with them. Maybe that sentiment is bouncing around inside my brain; I can't say for sure. I just know that I suck at goodbyes.

Where am I going with all of this? Today I have to say goodbye to Krischan.

Cindy, Justin and I are in Texas to celebrate Krischan's fourth birthday (which actually will be tomorrow, but his party is today). Krischan has spent the past 24 days with us, and although we're all pretty much exhausted from three weeks of movies, games, zoos, restaurants, cartoons and general good old-fashioned fun, it still pains me to say goodbye, which is what I will ultimately have to do at the end of the day.

Krischan's birthday party had a dinosaur theme, and I'll be the first to say it was a huge success. Both the kids and the adults had a terrific fun-filled day complete with cake, balloons, lunch… and of course presents. I gave Krischan a plastic moon--equipped with a remote control to light up the moon's various stages--to hang on his bedroom wall. The moon was a way of killing four birds with one stone: (1) Krischan is fascinated with all things outdoors; (2) Krischan expressed a desire to 'go to the moon with G-Pa.' When I told him it was far, far away he said we could get there if we rode on an airplane (he rode in an airplane for the first time when he flew into Atlanta a little over three weeks ago); (3) Krischan has a slight fear of the dark, and the moon in any of its 'lit' stages could serve as the nightlight he insists on sleeping with; and (4) the moon would serve as a constant reminder of (1), because if there's a way for us to fly to the moon before I die, we will. After all, he made me promise and all good G-Pa's keep their promises.

We capped off the day with dinner at a local barbecue joint. Krischan was genuinely thrilled when our waitress brought him a brownie smothered in vanilla ice cream and hot fudge with a single lit candle on top and the entire restaurant sang 'Happy Birthday' to him. Of course he blew out the candle and made a wish… for the second time today. After dinner we took a few more photographs (bringing the total for the day to roughly 2,000 or so) before we had to say our goodbyes to our four-year old bundle of joy.

Fortunately for this G-Pa, the occasion was so festive, so uplifting and so exciting that the one final hug and kiss I got from Krischan, along with him saying 'thank you for everything' didn't bring me to tears. My secret? I got it out of my system earlier in the day when I went for my morning run. Well, actually I just got out what was left in my system following my run from the day before, but I digress. I lifted Krischan up for that last hug after he—for the 100th or so time the past three weeks asked me to pick him up. Cindy urged me not to pick him up, as she knows my back isn't in very good shape. But I picked him up anyway, because there's no better feeling in the world than when he plants his cheek firmly against mine and just holds it there for several minutes at a time. I told Cindy there would be a time when he would no longer want me to pick him up, and for now I was taking every opportunity to do so, bad back or not.

Krischan has no idea how much joy and love he has brought into my life. I hope when he is old enough to read these words he'll realize the impact he had on my life.

As Cindy, Justin and I drove back to our hotel Cindy asked Justin if he was OK. Justin said he was. It never occurred to me that there might be someone who had more difficulty saying goodbye to the little guy than me. I guess that knocks me down a level on the 'good father' scale. But I hope I've earned an upgrade on the 'good grandfather' scale.

I saw a commercial back at the hotel room for an investment company. I know I've taken a few pot shots at the lack of imagination in advertising, but I will have to give one commercial a lot of credit. It showed an older gentleman in his office, moments after his retirement party. The accompanying words were something along the lines of 'You're leaving the only job you've ever loved.' Then it showed the same man playing with his granddaughter, the accompanying words this time being 'For the only job you've ever wanted.'

Exactly.

You can call me 'Little Tebow'

While we try to teach our children all about life,
Our children teach us what life is all about.
-Angela Schwindt

Today is only Yesterday's Tomorrow

March 2013

Today is only yesterday's tomorrow.

While I wish I could take credit for saying it, I have to give credit where credit is due. It's from *Circle of Hands*, a song from my youth written by Uriah Heep. What made me think of it was a conversation Cindy had with Krischan's mother yesterday.

Cindy checked in with her to see how Krischan was readjusting to being home in Texas after spending over three weeks with us in Georgia. She said Krischan was doing just fine, but had been asking her every day when he would be returning to Georgia. Long story short: Krischan was told he would be returning in August… in a few months… not too far in the future. You get the idea.

Then Cindy had this to say about that: In Krischan's mind the past, regardless of how long ago it may be is 'yesterday,' and anything in the future, regardless of how far off it may be is 'tomorrow.'

That caused me to think. What a wonderful world it would be if that were the case.

If the past was indeed yesterday, today:

Cindy and I would be feeling the lingering excitement of holding hands for the first time, kissing for the first time, slow dancing for the first time.

Would be our first day as husband and wife; newlyweds forever.

The ink on our high school diplomas would still be wet, as would the ink on our college diplomas.

The births of our two sons and our lone grandson would still be fresh in our minds.

Our carpet would have a light layer of black hair courtesy of our beloved Labrador Retriever Magic.

Maui, Molly, Millie, Moe and Morgan would still be kittens.

I would still be able to hit a golf ball straight and run a decent marathon.

Cindy and I would be sleeping in after a late night out on the dance floor.

And if the future was indeed tomorrow, today:

Everyone in the family would be going to bed tonight excited about Santa's arrival.

Cindy and I would be looking forward to being grandparents for the second time.

We would be losing sleep over the anticipation of the weddings of our children, our grandchildren and our great-grandchildren.

Cindy and I would be looking forward to retirement.

We would be planning how to spend the rest of our lives together. Truly together, not 'I'll see you for an hour or so after work' together but 'We have the entire day in front of us' together.

Today is only yesterday's tomorrow--courtesy of Uriah Heep.

Yesterday is the past; the future is tomorrow--courtesy of my grandson Krischan.

I have to admit, I like Krischan's better. It's such a refreshing, optimistic and hopeful spin on things.

My shirt says 'hungry'…because I am

Children seldom misquote. In fact, they usually repeat word for word what you shouldn't have said.
-Author Unknown

Missing Krischan

April 2013

Some days I need a Krischan fix. Today is one of those days. That can only mean one thing: Since I can't be with him I'm going to write about him. It's good for the soul... *my* soul. Here goes...

I love listening to my grandson Krischan talk. As Art Linkletter used to say: 'Kids say the darndest things.' Being around Krischan, I can really appreciate Mr. Linkletter's observation.

Some of Krischan's more memorable lines were spoken shortly after he turned three years old:

One weekend he was spending the night with Cindy and I. After his dad dropped him off I asked him if he had any underwear with him (since he was spending the night). He said yes and I asked him where they were.

His reply:

In my pay-ants (pants, but said with a distinct southern drawl).

Krischan got a small suitcase on wheels for a birthday present that his mom uses to pack his belongings when he spends the weekend with us. The first time he came to visit he rolled it around the kitchen a few times before announcing 'I'm leaving' and heading towards the garage. On his way to the garage he bent over and picked up one of his toy automobiles while adding:

I'm taking the car. (For those in the house who did
not see him bend over to pick up his toy automobile,
this took on an entirely different meaning.)

Cindy bought Krischan a chocolate pastry for breakfast one morning.
To enhance the dining experience, the waitress placed it in the microwave
for a few seconds. Big mistake. Chocolate everywhere: hands, face, shirt,
hair, etc. I asked Krischan what he was eating and he offered a reply that
made me wonder why I had never heard it before now:

A chocolate tastry.

Krischan (like Linus in the 'Charlie Brown' comic strip) has a security
blanket. Actually, it's more of a security 'sheet.' He carries it with him
everywhere so naturally he sleeps with it as well. One Saturday night he
spent the night with us and I woke up early Sunday morning and put the
sheet in the washing machine. I then went into the room where he was
sleeping to get my running gear to go for a run when Krischan suddenly
awoke from a deep sleep, sat up in bed, realized his sheet was missing and
asked:

Where's my sheet? Did the cats eat it?

In my world of being G-Pa, Krischan has taken the place of E. F.
Hutton.*

For the younger generation, this is a reference to the advertising slogan
of the E. F. Hutto, a former American stock brokerage firm:

When E. F. Hutton talks, people listen.

You say you haven't heard of it? I bet if you're a G-Pa you've heard it…

This is my 'bad boy' look

Kids: They dance before they learn there is anything that isn't music.
-William Stafford

Under the Stars

August 2013

It's been a while since Cindy and I have been on a picnic. It's been even longer since we've been on a picnic at night. So that made tonight the first of its kind since we enjoyed Gator Tails from Joe's Deli and a six-pack of ice-cold beer on the lawn in front of the student union for a Sunday night concert, a tradition while we were undergraduates at the University of Florida.

The differences between tonight and those nights of almost 40 years ago were many. The Gator Tail, six-pack and concert were now a turkey sub, a couple of Diet Cokes and a movie. Another difference? Our backs are no longer able to hold up sitting on a blanket for two hours. We were barely 20 in college; today?... well, do the math.* One more? We had a very special someone with us, and I'm here to tell you he had the time of his life.

I said that for Cindy's sake. I have no problem telling you I'm 58.

I'll leave Cindy's age a mystery. Give it a go, Nancy Drew.

What rambunctious four-year old wouldn't enjoy picking out the meal for the evening, watching an animated movie (*The Croods*) with his grandparents and generally being treated like a prince for several hours? Certainly not Krischan.

Krischan loved it. As an added bonus at the point in the night when *his* back was growing tired from sitting on the blanket, he had good ole G-Pa to lean back on. Apparently all the jumping up and down in the 'bounce house' before the movie took a little more out of him than he was counting on. Then again, maybe it was the field trip his Yia-Yia took him on earlier in the day to see the dinosaur exhibit at the Fernbank Science Center in Atlanta, or perhaps working with her at her store for a few hours later in the afternoon. Krischan somehow managed to make it to the end of the movie, but it was only a couple of minutes after we got home before he was out for the night. I can't say I blame him after the busy day he had.

Its nights like these I wish being a grandparent was a legitimate vocation.

Its nights like these I wish there were more nights like these.

It's nights like these I wish being four years old could last a lifetime; at least the lifetime of a certain set of grandparents who had the time of *their* lives seeing their four-year old grandson having the time of his life.

After all, isn't that what grandparents are *supposed* to do?

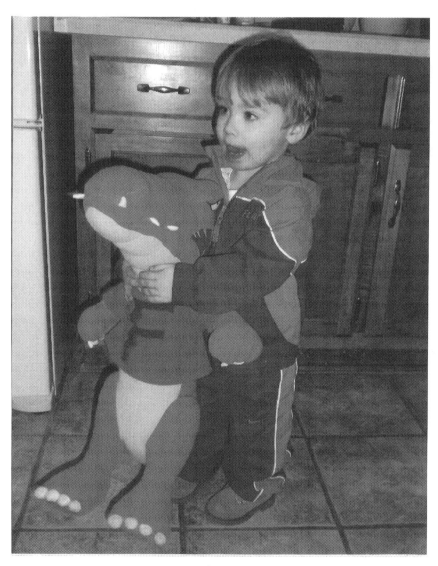

Me and my mascot

Grandchildren don't stay young forever, which is good
because Pop-pops have only so many horsey rides in them.
-Gene Perret

Let's call it a Day

August 2013

Yesterday Krischan and I squeezed as much as we could into 16 hours—including a much-needed 90-minute nap at halftime so we had the energy to make it through the fourth quarter. I'll be paying for it for the next couple of days, no doubt, so I'd best get my thoughts written down before any permanent damage sets in.

We began the day with a morning trip to Valerie's 40-acre property in Senoia. Krischan held a real live chicken for the first time in his life, and the surprise on his face when the chicken decided it no longer wanted to be held was quite the sight. 'You said chickens couldn't fly, G-Pa.' Translation: The chicken frantically flapped its wings to pry itself loose from Krischan's grasp and floated to the ground, creating the illusion of flying to a boy a bit shy of four-and-a-half years old. Pretend you opened a closet at home and found yourself face-to-face with a zombie. The look on your face would be the adult equivalent to the look on Krischan's face when the chicken began 'flying.' Or the look on my face when I was awoken 15 hours later from a sound sleep by the sound that strikes fear into the hearts of G-Pa's around the world.

A golf cart ride around the property, including a stop by the blueberry bushes for an impromptu all-you-can-eat buffet in blue was next on the agenda, followed by Krischan's examination of the three box turtles Val has raised since she found them breaking out of their shells on the path through the woods behind her house.

Next was a trip into downtown Senoia, or 'Woodbury,' as it is known to fans of the hit television series *The Walking Dead*. We visited the Woodbury

Shoppe, where you can find the officially licensed merchandise of the AMC show. I noticed all of the major stars of the show signed one of the walls and included a message to all of their fans. My Favorite was written by the character known as Tyreese: 'I must be the only black man to ever break into prison,' a nod to the fact that the survivors on the show have all taken refuge in an old abandoned prison to protect themselves from the zombies, or as they are known 'the walkers.'

About 10 minutes before any of the shops in Senoia would be open for business Krischan suddenly started bouncing up and down, adding that he needed to go to the bathroom… NOW! OK, this was new to me, since the last time we spent time together he would calmly mention he needed to go to the potty, essentially giving me a two-minute warning before the situation turned critical. Apparently now Krischan holds it until the very last second and breaks out in a dance that could easily be called 'the pogo stick.' So I looked for the nearest bush or tree, but Krischan would have no part of it. He wanted to use an *indoor* toilet, which is odd since earlier he had no problem 'watering the bushes' at Val's (sorry Val—if it's any consolation it wasn't the blueberry bushes). Then again there wasn't a lot of foot traffic at Val's at 8:30 a.m. Just before 11 a.m. in Senoia, now a tourist trap due to the success of *The Walking Dead* is a different story. Fortunately the hostess at one of the local eateries was kind enough to answer my frantic knock at the door and allow Krischan to use the facilities. I thought it was very kind of her and only wish Krischan hadn't said 'How come there aren't any customers; isn't the food here good?' on our way out.

On the way to get Krischan new shoes (it seems his shoe size changes with every full moon) he suddenly started having trouble breathing through his nose because it had 'too many boogers in it,' otherwise known as a runny nose. I handed him a tissue but he didn't appear to have a grasp on the concept of blowing his nose unassisted. I pulled over and literally gave him a hand and learned I have a talent for teaching children how to blow their very own nose (not at all as easy at it sounds).

We stopped for lunch and since I was needed for the two-person nose-blowing competition that was still in full swing, my appetite left a lot to be desired. We found a water fountain—the kind for tossing coins into and making wishes, a concept I explained to him—and handed him a penny and asked him to make a wish. He wished for 'a flower' and threw the penny into the water so hard it barely made a splash. Immediately he asked if I had another penny (I did. G-Pa's come prepared.). As I handed it to him I asked him to make a different wish and not to say it out loud. He again wished out loud for 'a flower' and threw the penny once again into the water so hard it barely made a splash. He asked for another penny and this time he wished—out loud, of course—for something a little more realistic: that he could go back to G-Pa's house and rest because he was tired.

When we got home Krischan and I took a 90-minute nap (see, that didn't take long): one of us desperately needed a nap and one of us desperately *wanted* a nap. (Discuss amongst yourselves whom needed what.) Afterwards we made a batch of sugar cookies and a batch of peanut butter cookies. I used the verb 'made' rather than 'baked' because the cookie dough came from a refrigerated package and all we had to do was roll it into balls and place them on an ungreased cookie sheet and bake for 12 minutes at 350 degrees.

I put Krischan in the bathtub so he could play with his rubber whale family (a mother and her three calves; now you can say you learned something today and don't you dare say you didn't) and wash off some of the chicken poop he had somehow managed to absorb earlier in the day. After a quick shower of my own we were both dressed and ready to head over to the Brickhouse for our regular Wednesday night music trivia. Krischan enjoyed seeing 'the regulars' on my team, all of them having known him since the day he was born. As you might imagine, his cookies were a hit with everyone as he proudly told anyone who would listen 'I made the cookies' while raising both arms above his head as his exclamation point. At the end of the night Cindy's business partner Tracey was pummeling Krischan with spitballs shot from a straw, and he was enjoying every second of it. Ahhh, kids.

It didn't take long once we got back home to get to bed. I was content knowing I was about to get almost six hours of sleep before the alarm would sound at 4 a.m. as I was meeting Al at his house for a 10-mile run at 5:30. When I was awoken at midnight with the sound of Krischan running to the bathroom, this time without doing the pogo because this time he was throwing up, I knew there was no hope of me getting much more than three or at best four hours sleep. You see, when Krischan throws up I've learned that it usually happens in three's. I was grateful he made it to the toilet before he started unloaded about half a dozen of his afternoon creations into it.

The second time I wasn't so lucky. Even though Cindy had placed a plastic bowl at bedside, Krischan bypassed it and headed straight to the bathroom, only to stop *one step shy* of the tiled bathroom floor before he deposited the other half-dozen cookies on the carpet so G-Pa would have something to look forward to before drifting back off to sleep. The third time? Pretty non-eventful, since the plastic bowl was used as intended.

We finally managed to fall asleep, a good thing considering we had another full day planned for the next day.

The day G-Pa asked me to help him write this book

There are no seven wonders of the world in the eyes of a child.
There are seven million.
-Walt Streightiff

The Butterfly

August 2013

One of Krischan's favorite things to tell me is that a caterpillar will one day turn into a 'beautiful butterfly.' One of the great joys in life for me is waiting to see what he'll say next. Today he didn't disappoint.

Seeing as Krischan and I would be spending the day together, he kept referring to it as 'our day.' I found it a bit strange since we spent all of yesterday together as well and I wasn't sure what distinguished this particular day as 'our day' while yesterday was simply 'Wednesday.' Perhaps it was because yesterday Krischan had to 'share' me with my music trivia team, while today he had me all to himself.

We ran into a woman I know who asked Krischan if he was going to be going to school this year and he proudly announced 'Yes I am' (he isn't). Then she asked him what his first day of school would be and without missing a beat he said with the utmost confidence and certainty 'the twenty-fourth.' I immediately thought how he just learned to count to 10 and wondered how he even knew about 'the 24th' and that the 24th was actually a Saturday so at best he had to have his dates confused.

Krischan asked if we would be going to any more 'penny fountains' because he had some more wishes he needed (not 'wanted,' but 'needed') to make.

We got caught in the rain. Krischan said it was 'raining bullets' and they were trying to hit us.

On the one or two occasions Krischan needed a reminder that I was the G-Pa and he was the grandson who should be listening to what his G-Pa tells him, he made mention that my 'brain is mean.'

We went to the movie theater and saw *Planes*, an animated film Krischan found fascinating (OK, so maybe I did as well). We shopped for Ninja Turtle underwear (for him; I prefer the superhero kind) prior to the movie; I wanted him to be prepared if in fact he would be starting school on the 24th.

When we got home we made another batch of cookies (Krischan's favorite: chocolate chip). He ate his fair share when we took them out of the oven. I didn't blame him one bit; after all, I was young once. (According to Krischan, I am *still* young. He thinks I'm six. Now that he knows what 24 is, I thought I would be at least that.)

I taught Krischan the difference between left and right so that when he saw Cindy later in the day he could point them out to her (she has trouble making the distinction). The three of us were in the car later (I was driving, Cindy was in the front passenger seat and Krischan was in his child seat in the back) and when we were at a stop light I asked Krischan which way we needed to turn to go home. He pointed decisively to the left and said 'left' and less than a minute later we were at a stop sign and he pointed decisively to the right and said 'right.' Cindy was amazed not only to learn which way was left and which way was right, but that Krischan could serve as a GPS if we needed him to. Then Krischan pointed up—and I know he was doing it to jokingly mock his Yia-Yia--and said 'up' and pointed down and said 'down.' I was laughing so hard my stomach was hurting. I'm pretty sure Cindy wanted to hit me in the stomach so it could hurt even more.

Today I discovered another of my great joys in life: Watching Krischan turn into a beautiful butterfly.

Being ring bearer wears a boy out

Children are the living messages we send to a time we will not see.
-Neil Postman

Literary Time Capsule

August 2013

After spending three weeks with Krischan, I thought it might be interesting—if not downright fun to ask him a few questions and record his answers so that one day he could look back and see how his mind worked when he was not quite four-and-a-half years old. I can't say for sure how Krischan will feel about it 20 years from now, but I can certainly say it was not only a lot of fun for me but quite interesting as well. Judge for yourself:

Q: What is your favorite movie?

A: *Hotel Transylvania* if you watch it with me, G-Pa because there is a really scary part in it and I want you to be here with me.

Q: How about if I'm not watching the movie with you? Then what is your favorite?

A: *Hotel Transylvania*. I'm not scared of it because I'm a big boy. It doesn't scare me. It doesn't. (This is a new habit he's developed; repeating himself to emphasize a point. The immediate contradiction of something he said earlier? That's an old habit.)

Q: What is your favorite color?

A: What is your favorite color, G-Pa? Blue? Mine too. Then orange and then green. Are those your next two favorite colors, G-Pa? (I say 'yes.') Then they're mine too.

Q: What is your favorite animal?

A: A seat pet. (There is a commercial for them on the television at the exact moment I ask this question; he's very open to the power of suggestion.)

Q: (After the commercial) What is your favorite animal?
A: A T-Rex. (See what I mean?)

Q: What is your favorite animal that is not extinct? (Yes, he knows what 'extinct' means.)
A: A gator. (Cindy and I have trained him well.)

Q: What is your favorite toy?
A: Gators! (Krischan has somewhere in the neighborhood of 50 gators—plastic, rubber, stuffed, etc. and he plays with ALL of them.)

Q: What is your favorite sport?
A: Gators! (He's referring to Florida Gator football.)

Q: What is the favorite sport you like to do?
A: Run! (I've trained him well.)

Q: What is your favorite cartoon?
A: *Scooby-Doo.*(Fact: I have seen every single *Scooby-Doo* cartoon. More than once.)

Q: What is your favorite fruit?
A: Blueberries! (I truly believe that boy might just bleed blue one of these days.)

Q: What is your favorite drink?
A: Choklit milk. (Pronounced *precisely* as it is spelled.)

Q: What is your favorite game?
A: Hide and Seek. (I love the way he plays. He asks me to close my eyes and count to 10 before telling me 'I'm going to go hide in the closet in your bedroom' or 'I'm going to be hiding in the shower.' Krischan believes his G-Pa is really good at playing Hide and Seek.)

Q: Who is your favorite superhero?

A: Spiderman and Hulk. (I'm having a hard time with this one, seeing as it wasn't long ago that Krischan gave me a T-shirt with 'Grandpa. This is what a REAL superhero looks like.' on the front of it.)

Q: What is your favorite shape?

A: A rectangle. (About a year prior Krischan asked me if our house was shaped like a rectangle. I told him yes and he said 'I like rectangles.' Apparently he still does.)

Krischan, I hope you'll appreciate this when you're in your 20's. I also hope I'll be around to run with you and watch *Scooby-Doo* cartoons with *your* children. After all, isn't that what Great-G-Pa's are for?

I'm in heaven!

A grandparent is old on the outside but young on the inside.
-Author Unknown

Second Wind

August 2013

I wanted to wait a few days before writing this.

I think I want to run another marathon.

I ran my 200th and final marathon last December 9 in Honolulu, Hawaii. I had been on a downward descent—both physically and mentally with my running for several years and reached the point where running marathons wasn't nearly as much fun as it used to be. In fact the last three or four marathons had been much more work than play. It was time for me to gracefully bow out of running marathons and make way for the young guns, which at this point in my life is anyone 55 or younger (yes, I know I'm only 58 but three years makes a huge difference).

But six days ago that all changed when I found something I had been missing for the past six years: My enthusiasm for running. I have my grandson to thank.

Last Thursday I bought Krischan a pair of running shoes (Stride Rites: not the flash-when-they-strike-the-ground model but the honest-to-goodness *running* model) and when we got home I was immediately hit with 'G-Pa, I want to run with you.' That had the exact same effect on me when my younger son Josh would say 'Dad, I'm going to go run—will you go with me?' about a generation ago. That is to say, I had my running shoes on in a matter of seconds.

Soon Krischan and I were out the door, at first running at a rapid pace as we hit the downhill slope of our cul-de-sac and then slowing as we reciprocated and went uphill a few minutes later. Krischan asked me to hold his hand while we ran: I'm assuming it's because his mother has done a good job of making sure he takes an adults' hand for safety when he's out in public, but it wouldn't surprise me if he took my hand so I wouldn't fall too far behind. After all his G-Pa isn't what he used to be; in fact, Krischan didn't even know his G-Pa *when* he 'used to be' because six or seven years ago he hadn't been born yet.

We ran, walked and ran aimlessly along the golf cart paths and through the neighborhoods of Peachtree City without any predetermined route to follow or time to finish by. This was the way running *should* be, and it was FAN-TAS-TIC. Krischan loved every second of it, whether he was acting as our 'coach' and telling us when to run and when to walk or when he deferred those duties to me. We stopped to pet every dog, smell every flower and read every sign (well, he asked me to read the signs to him). He stopped to introduce me to every single person we encountered as 'G-Pa,' eliciting a smile from each and every last one of them. He made sure they all noticed his brand new running shoes as well.

When we headed back up the cul-de-sac towards the end of our run/walk—after an hour and 45 minutes of the most fun I've had in quite some time, Krischan asked if we had 'run far.' I told him we had gone very, very far but in my mind I was thinking he couldn't possibly comprehend where he had taken me in our 105-minute journey.

Krischan made running fun again. I have the same perspective now I had in 1978, the first time I went for a run in Piedmont Park in Atlanta. I think I want to run another marathon.

Let's see what the neurosurgeon has to say for me about that subject when I see him in five days. I have my fingers crossed; I have Krischan to thank.

Anyone who thinks the art of conversation is
dead ought to tell a child to go to bed.
-Robert Gallagher

Photo Opp

August 2013

Confession time: When Krischan is around I become a camera-happy fool. A four-hour visit from Krischan easily translates into 50 or 60 candid photos of my favorite subject, my grandson. In the first three years of Krischan's life I imagine I took well over 2,000 photographs of him. I took photos of him the day he was born; in fact the very first photo of him is included in my second book. Several of my other books have featured photos of Krischan as well. He is even featured on the cover of one of my books. So far I have two albums dedicated to 8 X 10 enlargements of Krischan. There are framed photos of Krischan all over our house, as well as on the walls of the offices of both Cindy and I. Krischan's photo is the screen saver of my iPad and both my home and office computer. I've spent so much money on photographs the last four years the local Target's photography studio will no doubt one day bear my name

I've done a good job of providing all of our close relatives with photos of Krischan as well. It's not an exaggeration to suggest that Cindy's two brothers, her godparents and my sister all have as many photos of Krischan as most mothers have of their very own child. Now that Krischan has been living in Texas (over 600 miles away!) for over a year the photos may be farther in-between but not necessarily fewer. In fact I'm getting ready to send a stack of photos to all of them tomorrow along with this letter written by Krischan (with a little help from his G-Pa):

Hello,

It's me, Krischan! I just spent three weeks in Georgia and I wanted to tell you all about it. G-Pa and Yia-Yia stopped in Fort Worth to pick me up and take me on an airplane back to Atlanta. (Grammy—I used the *Cars* suitcase you gave me for Christmas two years ago; the one with the wheels on the bottom. I love it!) I really like flying on airplanes. I don't think G-Pa likes it as much as I do because he seems to sleep a lot while I spend all my time looking out the window at the clouds and the sky.

Yia-Yia took me to her store one day and I helped with some of the customers. It's important to have someone there to tell them where the restroom is and how old I am. No one ever asks Yia-Yia how old she is, but I'm pretty sure she's at least six because I have a friend who is five and Yia-Yia is bigger than her. Yia-Yia likes it when I tell her she is beautiful; I can tell because it makes her smile real big.

Yia-Yia also took me to see some dinosaur bones at a museum. They were real big, especially the one with the real long neck that eats leaves; you know, like a giraffe but only a dinosaur. (It's called a brontosaurus but I didn't think you would know that so I compared it to a giraffe instead.) I had a good time with the dinosaur bones, but it makes me sad that the real dinosaurs are extinct (and like I told G-Pa: Yes, I know what 'extinct' means).

Yia-Yia and G-Pa took me on a picnic. I picked out the sub sandwiches (I had turkey and avocado) and G-Pa and Yia-Yia shared one made out of turkey, lettuce and tomato. I liked mine better. I spent about ten minutes in a bouncy-house but G-Pa wouldn't do it with me because he said he didn't want to take his shoes off. The three of us sat on a blanket to watch the movie, *The Croods*. There were lots of dinosaurs in the movie, so it must have been made before they were extinct.

I went to church with Yia-Yia and G-Pa two times while I was in Georgia. The people I know told me they always ask about me when I'm in Texas and they seem glad to see me. One nice lady named Lori whom I have known for years took her puppet Lamb Chop out of her purse. Lamb Chop talked to me and gave me some candy; it seems like Lamb Chop always has candy for me!

G-Pa took me to his workhouse one day and I got to visit with everyone. They said I've grown a lot since the last time they saw me, but I don't feel any bigger and my clothes still fit. But now that I think about it, I have different clothes now so maybe I am bigger. I just didn't feel me growing so I can't say for sure.

I also spent two full days with G-Pa. I called them 'our days.' We went to a farm and I got to hold real live chickens except when one started flapping its wings and scared me and I let it go. But don't worry: It didn't fly away. I think the chicken was too fat to fly very far. We rode all over the farm on a golf cart but I didn't drive because like I told G-Pa I'm not allowed to drive yet. I think you have to be at least six to be able to drive, and I'm still only four. We went shopping for shoes and I got a pair of running shoes and a pair of sandals. We went to see *Planes* at the movie theater and I had a big bag of pakkarn and a fruit punch. I don't think G-Pa liked the movie as much as I did because he didn't seem too mad when I asked him to take me to the restroom. When we got home G-Pa and I went for a long run. We stopped to talk to every person and pet every dog we saw. G-Pa said we ran and walked about two miles. I don't know how far that is but I know that afterwards I took a shower (by myself!... but with G-Pa's help) and then fell asleep on the chair with G-Pa pretty fast (he fell asleep, too). After all we had two pretty big days!

I played music trivia with G-Pa and Yia-Yia two times and only fell asleep one of the times. I'm not too much help to them with music trivia unless a Beatles song is played, because I know my Beatles. The waitress there is real nice to me and always lets me make up my own dinner from all of the different foods on the children's menu. One night I had pakkarn shrimp, chicken strips and fries—three of my favorites. The night I fell asleep Yia-Yia took one of my shrimps so when I woke up I let her know I knew she did it.

I spent a lot of time with my Daddy, too. Daddy and I exercise together because he has big muscles and I do too. We went for pizza a couple of nights to one of my favorite restaurants, Chuck E. Cheese. I saw Chuck both times we were there and it seems like he remembered me from my last trip to Atlanta. The most fun was when we had battles in Daddy's back yard with squirt guns! I won every time except when Daddy squirted me in my eye and it made me cry. But I didn't cry for long because Daddy had dinner waiting for me and my stomach was hungry more than my eye was hurting.

The four of us flew back to Texas on an airplane and I spent the first night in a hotel with them. We ate a big breakfast and G-Pa made me a waffle that was shaped like Texas. It tasted like any other waffle; it just wasn't square. I had to go to the emergency room that afternoon because I had a hard time walking and everyone was afraid because I didn't fall or get hit by anything and they couldn't understand why my leg hurt. The doctors were nice and gave me ice cream and said I was OK after they took pictures of my leg with a big machine that said 'bzzzz.' G-Pa thinks I may have slid off my chair at the Mexican restaurant the first night we were in Texas and it made my leg muscle stretch too far. But my leg was feeling better before everyone flew back to Atlanta.

I'm going to miss them but they said I would see them again real soon. I hope you like the pictures!

Love,

Krischan

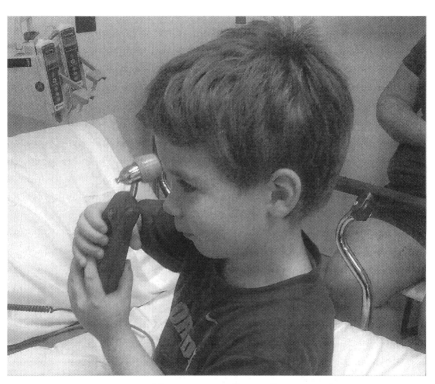

Self-examination (I was fine)

If you haven't time to respond to a tug at your
pants leg, your schedule is too crowded.
-Robert Brault

Sometimes It can be a Bit Much

March 2014

Today was unlike any other, at least for me. If you've got a grandson, a cat or two with sensitive stomachs and a non-inflated Spiderman 2 punching bag you might possibly have had a day like this. If so, just play along. For everyone else, brace yourselves:

My grandson Krischan and I just returned home from a 90-minute run/walk/oh-look-at-the-ducks! excursion and I tried loading a game on his Leapfrog tablet (a children's version of an iPad, as far as I can tell) using a gift card he got for his 5th birthday two days earlier. It wasn't long before I called Leapfrog's help line, where I was told again and again by a pre-recorded electronic Mary Poppins that my wait to speak to someone would require 'a minimum wait of 10 minutes.'

In other words, allowing me plenty of time to play with Krischan and his new Spiderman 2 punching bag, another of his birthday presents that apparently requires adult intervention. Please note (a) the word 'new,' indicating the punching bag was still in its original 8-inch by 10-inch box and needed to be inflated and (b) there was virtually no difference between the Spiderman 2 punching bag and the original Spiderman punching bag other than the numeral '2' after Spiderman's name. So I removed the non-inflated piece of black and blue rubber from the box and that's when the fun really began...

Because that is when I heard one of the cats tossing her Cat's Meow all over the dining room rug which meant I got to do my absolute favorite (Sarcasm Font) thing in the whole wide world other than being placed on hold on the telephone or inflating rubber punching bags: Clean up cat vomit.

So about the time I got to my knees to start 'picking up the pieces' (if you ever saw regurgitated Cat's Meow you'd understand) I heard Krischan calling out that he 'needs to go to the BAFFroom.' I noticed the urgency in his voice. Seconds later I noticed the urgency all over his shirttail. I asked him to take off 'anything wet' and took the wet garments into the laundry room where I threw everything into the washing machine. As it was a fairly new washing machine, I wasn't familiar with the ringing sound it was making.

Simple explanation: The ringing sound wasn't the washing machine; it was the front doorbell. So I ran to the door and peered through the glass panels and decided I didn't have any business with two men in their late 20's wearing white shirts and black ties and riding bicycles in 30-degree weather.

Krischan, however had other ideas. He walked up behind me, opened the front door and said hello to the two men. Butt nekkid, of course.

However, I seized the opportunity to make myself scarce. I screamed 'Sorry—emergency,' slammed the door in their faces, grabbed Krischan in all his naked glory and carried him upstairs to put on some dry clothes....

… only to hear the door bell ringing again. And again and again. Aggravated and ready to give the two men at my front door more than they bargained for, I stormed down the stairs, pulled the front door wide open with the rage of the Incredible Hulk etched all over my face and ready to unleash the wrath of the God of Thunder (I love Marvel comics) when the taller of the two men quietly said:

'We just wanted you to know your gray cat ran outside when your son opened the front door.'

Feeling foolish and to be honest a little bit flattered (see, they thought Krischan was my son) I ran out the front door like the Flash (D. C. comic book reference; sorry to confuse you) and started screaming for Millie (the gray cat), frantically scouring the bushes lining the front of the house.

Meanwhile, a certain naked little boy took the opportunity to grab his box of sidewalk chalk (in a variety of rainbow colors!) to demonstrate his inner Rembrandt all over the driveway, interrupting my search for Millie so I could grab Krischan before the neighbors called the police to report my negligence in the area of adult supervision. I grabbed Krischan with one arm and carried him on my hip as I approached the porch and felt a small bit of relief when I opened the front door with my free hand and saw Millie running hysterically back into the house. 'Gee,' I thought to myself. 'Just what I need: A traumatized cat.'

I noticed the telephone lying on the kitchen counter with the same elevator music playing when I was first put on hold, presumably a lifetime or two ago. A gentle feminine voice was telling me that my 'call was very important' and would be answered as soon as possible.

So while the good people in customer service at Leapfrog were diligently working towards an award for Performance of the Year (please appreciate my special Sarcasm Font), I took the opportunity to dress Krischan and resume Operation Inflation. After blowing into the rubber valve stem and having nothing to show for it, Krischan commented: 'It's not getting *bigger!*' Sadly he was right, which led right into my 'Aha!' moment: 'I'll take the punching back into the garage and inflate it with my electric air pump!' Great concept—the later addition of duct tape around the valve stem and the pump nozzle made it even greater. Before long I was face-to-face with a four-foot tall rubber Spiderman with only one discernable problem: He couldn't stand up straight. Checking the instructions (Instructions for a punching bag? Well of course!) I discovered there was another opening at the bottom that had to be filled 'with sand or water' to ensure Spiderman 2 would stand at attention and return to that position after being punched. I tried adding water by using a plastic cup in the kitchen, and once I got a couple of ounces of water into the punching bag and another couple of pounds of water on the kitchen floor, I had my second 'Aha!' moment: I'll take the punching bag outside and fill the base using the garden hose.' So after connecting the garden hose to the outside faucet, I stuck the end of the hose into Spiderman 2's bottom and filled it with water. OK, I lied because the pressure of the water caused the hose to pop loose from Spidey's butt and I had to reinsert the hose not once but twice until the connection was strong enough to hold.

Once Spiderman 2 was standing tall, I turned around to show Krischan and... *Krischan?* Now where could he be? Where all little boys go to stir up trouble when the last thing you need for them to do is stir up trouble: To visit a nest of red ants in the flowerbed. And by 'visit' I mean 'kick with every fiber of his being.' After brushing off all of the ants I could see on his shoes and pant legs I turned my attention elsewhere: To ME to brush off all of the ants I could see on MY shoes and pant legs. I then kicked off my shoes and removed Krischan's shoes and grabbed his hand and ran inside the house to spray some ointment on our respective red ant bites.

And clean up another splotch of recycled Cat's Meow.

In the background I heard a gentle feminine voice reminding me that my 'call was very important' and would be answered as soon as possible.

Krischan and I went outside where I took out my frustrations on Spiderman 2.

Grandfathers are just antique little boys.
-Author Unknown

That Little Boy Smell

March 2014

Everyone knows the smell. Anyone who has ever been around a small, energetic boy, that is.

The slight odor of dried perspiration, the feint hint of stale puppy dog breath and a sprinkle or two of good ole' dirt and grime for good measure. Yes, that would be the smell of a little boy after a full day of—well, being a little boy.

One generation removed from having two little boys of my own, I am now the proud G-Pa of an energetic, never-sit-or-stand-still grandson. Today we were going to do things little boys enjoy doing. Or as he told Cindy before she left for work: 'Today we're doing *man* things.'

First thing on the agenda: Hanging a wind ornament in the yard, a Christmas present I received last year from Yia-Yia. (It might have been three years ago, perhaps as many as five.) If I do say so myself: We did a great job and the ornament looks fantastic. It made me wonder what took me so long. It also made me wonder how much longer it would have taken had Krischan not insisted we hang it *today*.

Next came a trip to the store to buy some much-needed accessories for the day: Ice cream, a Tee-ball baseball glove, a collage-style picture frame, a two-pack of Teenage Mutant Ninja Turtle toothbrushes (one for G-Pa and Yia-Yia's house and one for Daddy's house) and enough boxes of Hot Tamales (or 'spicy candy,' as Krischan calls it) to keep our tongues in red dye for the rest of his three-week visit with us.

What would a trip to the store be without a stop at the Golden Arches* on the way home? (*A clever ploy on Krischan's part to make his way to

McDonald's indoor playground, one of his favorite respites. I fell for it. I always do.)

Once we got back home it was time to 'break in the leather.' But first things first: I had to explain how a right-handed boy should wear a baseball glove on his *left* hand; not nearly as simple as it sounds. Granted, Krischan may in time prove to be ambidextrous (he is equally adept at throwing things hard with both his right and his left hand) but for the sake of today's lesson I assumed he'll eventually be a pure righty. He managed with the glove for a while, up until the point his 'hand got sweaty' and he switched the glove over to his right hand. From that point on he was catching the ball in the web of the glove on his right hand (good) but trying to throw the ball back to me Jai-Alai style with the ball still in his gloved right hand (bad).

Now it was time for some 'man things,' meaning things I have done for many years but if I had my druthers someone else would be doing them. Like pulling weeds in the garden along the side of our yard. Or in this case, getting rid of the 'snake creatures' that were trying to infiltrate the garden along the side of our yard. Is there a better 'snake creature catcher' than a grandson? I think not! (Score one for G-Pa.)

Is there a better reward for a job well done for a five-year old boy than handing him a box of sidewalk chalk and telling him to go crazy on your driveway? If there is I'd like to know about it, because Krischan's face lit up like mine had 30 minutes earlier when I saw Krischan catch a ball in the web of his glove (which at the time was on the correct *left* hand) for the very first time in his life.

We took a break from the brilliant springtime afternoon sun and went inside to rummage through countless family photos until we found the perfect six—three horizontally framed and three vertically framed—to fit into the photo collage frame. It would be a gift for Papa, Krischan's great grandfather later in the day.

But before that, Krischan and I went for our afternoon run (and walk whenever Krischan's 'heart hurt'). We ran (and walked) by the usual spots: The lake on the 18th hole of the Braelinn Golf Course that is inhabited by a baby-duck-eating shark; the tunnel running beneath Braelinn Road 'where the Ninja Turtles live;' and the tool shed on the 2nd hole of the golf course 'where zombies sleep.' That grandson of mine has quite the imagination: That shark couldn't possibly discriminate between baby ducks and adult ducks, and did he even consider adolescent ducks? Seriously, sometimes that boy just doesn't think things through.

Our final stop of the day was the assisted living complex where Papa (Cindy's godfather) has been a resident for the past four months. Seeing Krischan brought a *huge* smile to Papa's face. As the three of us made our way out to the commons for a walk around the grounds I noticed Krischan had a similar affect on the entire Memory Care Unit, residents and staff alike. An effervescent five-year old boy and his infectious smile will do that to a person. After our walk we sat outside and enjoyed the bright sunshine and the cool afternoon breeze. I managed to snap a couple of photos of the two of them—separated in life by 83 years but today as close as a great-grandfather and great-grandson could possibly be. We escorted Papa to the dining hall for his dinner, me holding one arm and his great-grandson ever-so-carefully holding onto the other. Krischan only let go of his death-grip to run ahead and hold open any doors in our path.

When we returned home it was time for a bath. Krischan wanted to 'wash the sweat out of his hair' after a full day of being a boy.

After a day like today there is no doubt in my mind he had that little boy smell.

But you can't take my word for it. I couldn't tell.

Most likely because I smelled like a little boy, too.

I can always make Papa smile!

Having a grandson is like having a blender
that you don't have the top for.
-Jerry Seinfeld (with an assist by Scott Ludwig)

Yes Man

March 2014

After spending a lot of time the past three weeks with my grandson Krischan, I've become pretty familiar with his level of proficiency with the English language. I have to admit: For a barely five-year old boy, he's got quite the way with words. I especially like his go-to response on the rare occasion when I had to admonish him with an ever-so-slight reprimand: *'You hurt my heart.'* This, of course is then followed up with slouched shoulders and lips extending all the way down to his chin. It was all I could do to keep from chuckling out loud or at the very least giving him a great big hug.

One word that appears to have disappeared from Krischan's vocabulary is the word 'no.' In fact the only time I recall Krischan using it was after he jumped in the tub for a bath and I told him I wanted to wash his hair so he could relax and enjoy playing with his rubber dolphins until his toes started turning into prunes. If it wasn't for the fact that the shampoo (a) was tear-free, (b) smelled like watermelon and (c) featured SpongeBob SquarePants on the bottle, I probably wouldn't have stood a chance.

The word—other than 'G-Pa, of course—that I heard most often was simply: 'Yes.'

No matter what the question, the answer was always the same.

'Do you want to go for a really long run that will make us super tired?'

'Do you want to try a bite of this? It's really, really hot.'

'Do you want to go for a ride in the car with the top down even though it might rain and we'll get wet?'

'Do you want to throw a penny in the fountain and make a wish?'

'Do you want me to read a scary book to you?'

'Do you want to play catch? Throw the football? Shoot baskets?'

'Do you want to dig for worms? Look for ants? Chase the squirrels?'

"Do you want to take a walk in the woods and look inside the old shack where zombies probably live?'

'Do you want to get on a rocket ship and fly to the moon?'

The answer was always the same: 'Yes.'

The kid is one part adventurer, one part thrill-seeker and three parts fearless. And without a doubt, the kid is… 100% boy.

Several nights while Krischan was with us I was a bit surprised by something he said 'yes' to, seeing as 'no' was the answer I had been getting for the first five years of his life. After a rather full day of (as we called them) 'man things' I asked him just after 9 p.m. if he was ready to put on his Ninja Turtle jammies and go to sleep. You can imagine my surprise hearing the word 'yes' where the word 'no' used to dwell.

I learned a lot these past three weeks. I learned life can be more exciting when you're willing to take risks. I learned life is a lot more fun when you're willing to try new things. I learned life is a lot more— *exhilarating* when you're willing to put your fears aside and just go for it. No matter your age, there's a lot to be learned from an inquisitive, wide-eyed and willing-to-give-everything-and-anything-a-chance five-year old boy.

At 59 years of age, I've still got new things to learn.

I've still got new things to do.

Most of all, I've still got new things to *live*.

If you have any doubts, just ask Krischan.

My first slam dunk

*The real menace in dealing with a five-year old is that in
no time at all you begin to sound like a five-year old.*
-Joan Kerr

The Sidekick

August 2014

Krischan has called me G-Pa since he learned how to articulate words with more than one syllable.

> *G-Pa can I have a glass of choklit milk? G-Pa can we go
> running? G-Pa let's watch cartoons. G-Pa why do deer live in
> the forest and not in a house? G-Pa let's hunt zombies.
> G-Pa I had an ax-i-dent.*

That's why Krischan caught me off guard when he referred to me as his 'sidekick' a couple weeks ago.

We were out exploring in the woods behind my house when he said I needed to stay close to him because that's what a good sidekick does. *'You know, like Robin is to Batman,'* he added after misinterpreting the reason I was rolling my eyes.

I stayed close to Krischan as we got deeper and deeper into the woods, making sure no zombies, space aliens or wild animals were sneaking up on us from behind. Don't ever accuse me of not being a good sidekick; I know what needs to be done.

While there are no written rules and regulations for being a good sidekick (I checked), I have accumulated a partial list of what Krischan expects from me. After all, every Batman needs a good Robin:

- Know the answer to any and every question. Subject matter is irrelevant; just know EVERYTHING. *How does a chameleon know what color they should be? Why are they called 'stink bugs?' I don't smell anything. Do trees hurt when you chop them down?*

- Identify each of the Teenage Ninja Mutant Turtles by the color of their headbands.

- Sit through numerous viewings of *How to Train Your Dragon* and pretend each time you're seeing it for the very first time.

- Be ready for any and every physical activity after a long drive in the car. *(The fact that the sidekick did all the driving while someone else was taking a nap has no impact whatsoever on this requirement.)*

- Always have tissues handy. Even if caught in the middle of the woods during a heavy rain. (Trust me on this one.)

- Explain why 'tenteen' isn't a number when it makes perfectly good sense to him.

- Hold your own in the more popular games available on tablets, like Fruit Ninja and Angry Birds. That is, do everything you can to be competitive without actually winning. *(Save the winning for the teenage years when he'll need to be taught a lesson or two.)*

- Ensure he doesn't lick the shattered screen on a cell phone because he believes it to be 'covered in sugar.'

- Provide reassurance that even the greatest basketball player alive couldn't touch the rim at one time.

- Pretend to be amazed when he runs across the room and back, comes to a sudden halt and stands perfectly still while desperately trying not to breathe hard. Then acknowledge he has proven he is indeed the Flash, the fastest man alive.

- Always have his back while hunting zombies in the woods, with Styrofoam sword held firmly in both hands. Just in case.

- 'Go first' when entering a dark room. If it's nighttime, then always 'go first' when returning to the dark hallway.

Krischan will be spending the next few days with Cindy and I. That means I'll be stopping at the grocery store today on the way home to pick up a bottle of Krischan's favorite drink, chocolate milk.

Just like any sidekick worth his salt would do.

No, I'm not ready to come in for dinner!

Run when you can, walk if you have to, crawl
if you must; just never give up.
-Dean Karnazes

This 1812 was no War

September 2014

I don't know who was more excited this morning: My five-and-a-half year old grandson or me. But I do know this: We both had the time of our lives.

I've had the pleasure of running with Krischan pretty much since the day he learned to walk. The boy loves to run, and I couldn't be happier. Or prouder, seeing as he 'wants to run just like G-Pa.' In fact Krischan reminds me of my son/his Uncle Josh when he first started running a couple of decades ago. It's been quite a spell between generations, but after today I can honestly say it's been worth the wait.

You see, this morning Krischan ran his first official race and I had the pleasure of being there with him, every hop, step and detour-to-pick-up-miscellaneous-odds-and-ends (baseball, pine cone, dead cicada) along the shady, hilly one-mile route near Spalding Regional Hospital in Griffin, Georgia.

After a busy afternoon and evening yesterday hunting invisible space alien babies in the woods behind the house, finding a jawbone that instantly transformed us into 'scientists' (the 'fossil' was later identified by a Facebook friend as that of a deer) and baking our requisite Friday night batch of peanut butter cookies, I woke up this morning at 3:45 to get in my 10-mile run with my friend Al… while Krischan slept in until 7:30 (our race was at 9:00). Of course no five-and-a-half year old boy 'sleeps in' until 7:30; rather he was woken up early on this Saturday morning by his Yia-Yia to get ready for his racing debut. As you can imagine it wasn't pretty, but after he put on his shorts, shirt and 'running shoes' he couldn't wait to get to the starting line.

'How much further?' I heard more than once as we made the 30-minute drive to Griffin. When we pulled into the parking lot his eyes were as wide as the finishing medal he hoped to have draped around his neck once he crossed his first finish line. I didn't have the heart to tell him there probably wouldn't be a medal for the race (there was an accompanying 5K race—the 'big event;' the one-mile was merely the accompanying 'fun run') but if there wasn't he could choose one of mine when we got back to the house. (He's always admired my collection of running medals, and one day it is certain to be his.)

We picked up Krischan's race packet and he instantly asked me to pin his race number to the front of his shirt. The number almost covered his entire stomach but that didn't matter to him: He was now an 'official runner.' We walked back to the car to drop off his packet and although I had asked him several times just moments earlier if he needed to use the restroom while we were near the hospital and he said 'no' every time, once we were in the parking lot—with neither a rest room nor porta-pottie anywhere in site—he had to go. *'Now!'* He ran to a tree, dropped his shorts to his ankles and let it fly. It was hard to believe this was the same little boy whom I implored to 'water a tree' last summer in a similar emergency situation and he absolutely refused.

All I can figure is it must have been the pressure of running his first race. I asked him as we headed to the starting line what made him so bold; he didn't have an explanation, but as we got close to the gathering of runners he asked me if we could 'stop talking about this now?' After all, it was time to get down to business. Besides, it wasn't a good idea for G-Pa's to embarrass their grandsons by taking about their bathroom habits when they were about to compete in an athletic competition for the first time.

As we waited at the back of a pack of 100 or so runners (the 5K and the one-mile started simultaneously, but the two races took different routes) I told Krischan not to start out too fast because, after all, a mile is a really long way. Over the years Krischan has covered as many as three miles with me, but as you might imagine not all of it was running: There was always a good amount of walking, talking to neighbors and petting every dog that crossed our path. But today would be different: Today was all about *running*.

As the Race Director was going over the instructions for the races, Krischan asked if we could hold hands while we ran. 'You know, so you can keep up with me, G-Pa.' I told him he would need to have his hands free so his arms could pump as he ran, but I would do my absolute best to keep up with him.

Krischan started off exactly as I asked: Conservative pace, arms-a-pumping and cheeks turning bright red as he crested the first of several hills on one of the more challenging 'fun run' courses I've ever seen. Let me be the first to say the experience was wonderful: He smiled the entire time, slowed down only for a couple of steps because his 'stomach hurt' and even managed to squeeze in a little exploration and housekeeping along the way. Krischan waved to everyone along the course and got excited every time someone shouted him encouragement ('Do they know me, G-Pa? They must because they're cheering for me!').

We played leapfrog with several other runners for most of the race. As you probably already guessed I took my fair share of photos along the way so I could have a record of this special morning. As we neared the finish line, by my calculation we were in the middle of a pack of about 25 runners, walkers, moms, dads and one lone G-Pa. I told Krischan he should cross the finish line in front of me because I wasn't wearing a number, but he would have none of it: We would be crossing the finish line together. I think what he said was 'Catch up to me, G-Pa; I'll slow down so you can' which was his subtle way of reminding me I'm not as young as him (he currently thinks I'm 25, by the way).

We ran the final 10 or so glorious steps together and crossed Krischan's first finish line in an official time of eighteen minutes and twelve seconds. 18:12, a time that is now part of my vernacular along with 76:36 (a

10-mile race Josh ran when he was nine years old), 3:18:15 (Cindy's first half-marathon) and 36:14 (my 10K best). I imagine when my memory starts failing me—I'm guessing around the time I'm running my great-grandchild's first race with him or her—the time I'll still remember will be 18:12.

While Krischan may not remember his finishing time, I have high hopes that he'll always remember the day he ran just like his G-Pa.

Postscript: Six weeks later I paced Krischan in his second one-mile race. He ran—all 5,280 feet—and lowered his time by almost eight minutes, finishing in 12 minutes and 21 seconds.

The next time out he lowered his time to 11 minutes and 11 seconds.

It won't be long before he'll be running faster than his G-Pa.

I've got G-Pa's form!

What a bargain grandchildren are! I give them my loose change,
and they give me a million dollars' worth of pleasure.
-Gene Perret

Kid in the Hall

October 2014

Given the choice between a chocolate candy bar and a tomato, he'd opt for the healthier choice and grab the vegetable… and ask for seconds.

Given the choice between spending the day at the circus or a two-hour trip to the museum, dinosaur bones and prehistoric cave art trump red-nosed clowns and high-flying acrobats every time.

Given the choice between sitting on the couch to watch cartoons or going for a run, he'd rather lace up his tiny running shoes even though it would be much simpler to slip on a pair of tiny alligator bedroom slippers and watch some butt-stomping mutant turtles.

If I've learned one thing about my grandson Krischan, it's that he is prone to say or do the exact opposite of what most people would expect. You can include me in that category, even though by now I should know better. My wife Cindy and I took Krischan to Atlanta's brand new College Football Hall of Fame—through a special offer from the Atlanta Gator Club—and expected his tolerance level for 'all things football' to be somewhere in the neighborhood of four or five minutes. As our tour was scheduled to last two hours, our apprehension about taking Krischan with us is understandable.

A little background: Krischan has been exposed to 'all things Gator' since the day he was born. I won't go into detail but let's just say everything from his first onesie to his first stuffed gator to his first sippie cup has been orange and blue. He's been doing the Gator 'chomp' since he was two. He can instantly recognize the Gator football team when they're playing on

TV. And yes, he can yell 'Go Gators!' at the top of his lungs with the best of us. The boy was born to bleed orange and blue.

But two solid hours of NBF (nothing but football)? Was it too much for a boy not yet six years old? Let's find out, shall we?

4:00 – 4:05 p.m. We met our tour guide Terry LeCount, former NFL player and more importantly former Florida Gator. Terry was the quarterback at Florida when Cindy and I were students there. In fact Terry played quarterback in high school at Raines, one of the archrival schools in Jacksonville, Florida of Duncan U. Fletcher, the alma mater of Cindy and I. How did my high school fare in football against Terry's alma mater? Let's just say the Raines mascot was a Viking and the Fletcher mascot was a Senator: Now imagine the two of them squaring off. Yeah, it was ugly. Truth be known Fletcher Senior High was located at the beach and in a perfect world our school mascot would be Jeff Spicoli, the surfer dude from *Fast Times at Ridgemont High ('All I need are some tasty waves, a cool buzz and I'm fine.')*.

4:05 – 4:20 p.m. We listened to our special guest Danny Wuerffel, former NFL player, former Florida Gator and former Heisman Trophy Winner (1996). Danny led the Gators to four consecutive SEC Championships (1993 – 1996) and a National Championship in his senior year. Danny told some old war stories from his days playing for the 'Evil Genius,' former Florida Head Coach Steve Spurrier. Although I've heard the stories before I still find myself laughing—probably because Danny's impersonation of Spurrier is so spot-on accurate with his rat-a-tat delivery and scrunched up nose—that I can practically envision Steve himself up on the stage. My favorite story from Danny's repertoire (I'm paraphrasing here):

I was a freshman at Florida and pretty nervous playing in front of such a large crowd for the first time. I called a basic pass play that allowed the receiver a multitude (I counted seven as Danny spoke) of variations in the route he would be running. As I called the signals at the line I audibled to announce which of the routes the receiver should run. I threw the football exactly where the receiver should have been, but the receiver turned 'in' when he should have turned 'out' and the pass was intercepted. I was really afraid to go to the sideline because I feared what Coach would have to say; I was just hoping he realized the interception was the receiver's mistake and not mine. I ran up to him and said 'sorry, coach' and he replied back: 'It's not your fault, Danny. It's mine… for putting you out there in the first place.'

After Danny spoke we had the opportunity to meet him, but seeing how long the line was we opted for seeing a 10-minute video of what it's like on the sideline, in the huddle and on the field of an NCAA football game. Krischan seemed to like it because there was a fair share of Gator players throughout the film. Afterwards we returned to stand in a still fairly long line to meet Danny. Once we got to the head of the line Cindy got Danny's autograph on two posters we picked up on the way in (a cartoon alligator chasing after a cartoon bulldog—perfect since the annual Florida-Georgia game was only seven days away).

Krischan did Cindy one better. Danny picked him up, sat Krischan down next to him on the side of the stage, posed for a couple of photographs and spoke to him directly for a good 90 seconds. Looking at the photographs later, you would have thought Krischan was sitting on a nail rather than sitting next to a former Heisman Trophy Winner. All this time poor Danny was fighting a winless battle trying to coax a 'Go Gators!' out of him.

4:20 – 5:20 p.m. This was where Krischan's patience was put to the test. We were touring the actual Hall of Fame. (When Krischan saw all of the exhibits he asked me if we were now in the 'dinosaur moo-zeum.') Surprisingly there were plenty of things that appealed to him (most of it being the state-of-the-art interactive stations sprinkled throughout the hall). One of the stations took a photo of Krischan's face, displayed it on a screen and allowed him to paint it orange and blue and select from an assortment of Gator logos. Another allowed him to 'measure up' against a 6'6" Auburn football player (Krischan was a hair under 4'). The most interesting station were large touch-screen devices suspended from the ceiling that allowed you to revisit the legends of yesterday via historic footage, interviews and testimonials. Well, at least they *looked* interesting—between Cindy and I we have less technological know-how than most five-year olds so we were never able to navigate our way through the screen but we did manage to get an error message... on a computer screen that everyone else in the Hall didn't seem to have a problem with. I can't remember the wording on the error message, but it said something like this:

Remove your hand from the screen and walk away before you cause any irrevocable damage to this system. May we suggest giving your grandson a chance?

5:20 – 5:45 p.m. A small artificial-turf playing field is located on the first floor of the Hall. Krischan couldn't wait to get to it (he could see it from both the second and third floors where we had spent the first 80 minutes). This should be fun.

Activity #1: Throw three footballs at three holes in a large net from a distance of 20 yards. Translation for a five-year old: Throw three footballs with all your might in the general direction of the man in uniform standing beside the net, using two hands if the football is too large for one hand (it most definitely was). Krischan made three crisp two-handed floaters—with all his might--to the man in uniform who took the ball each time and slammed it into each of the three holes in the net, completing the finest and perhaps only trio of alley-oops in the history of football.

Activity #2: Run shoulder-first into a blocking sled, weave through eight tackling dummies and catch a pass while falling into a large foam cushion. Translation for a five-year old: Do what is necessary to avoid the blocking sled, run straight through eight tackling dummies and dive into a large foam cushion while a perfectly-thrown pass floats over your head.

Activity #3: Kick a 20-yard field goal from a tee. Translation for a five-year old: Run towards the football and do whatever is necessary to distinguish whatever you do to it from anything you might do to a soccer ball. This one was doomed from the start. Man in uniform (to Krischan): 'Left-footed or right-footed?' Krischan: (shrugs). Man: 'Left or right?' Krischan: (still shrugging from the first time). In the end it didn't matter—left or right—because when Krischan reached the ball and made contact with his right foot (I can't say he actually 'kicked' the ball, rather he 'moved the ball with the top of his foot') the football traveled about 10 yards along the ground. Disappointed he didn't 'kick the football between the yellow poles,' I told Krischan he made a good kick but the wind got hold of it.

Activity #4: Cornhole, where the object is to toss a beanbag into a small circular hole cut into a wooden ramp from a distance of 10 yards. Krischan chose me as his opponent. We made four sets of four throws; I managed to put one into the hole in each set ('Ooooh G-Pa, you DID it!' said with the excitement I wish he'd shown Danny Wuerffel a little over an hour ago). Krischan never got one of his beanbags in the hole, but he did manage to throw a beanbag sideways, backwards, straight up, three yards and 23 yards among his 16 tosses. While my throws were a lot more consistent, Krischan's throws were a lot more creative (and dangerous to anyone in the general vicinity of the cornhole area).

5:45 – 6:00 p.m. The last stop was the gift shop. Krischan spotted a small Florida Gator football, picked it up and asked if he could have it so he could play football with his G-Pa. The price tag was hefty—as you might expect in any moo-zeum—but you might say the odds were stacked heavily in Krischan's favor. My only grandson wanted a football—his first football and a *Gator* football, no less—so he could play with his G-Pa.

My American Express had about as much of a chance as Krischan's 20-yard field goal try.

When Cindy and I attended the University of Florida we didn't have very good football teams. In fact each season ended with cries of 'wait 'til next year.'

Wait 'til next year indeed. Krischan started practicing with his small Florida Gator football today. Next year I'll wager he'll be kicking the football 'between the yellow poles.'

Heisman trophy winners don't impress me much

To a small child, the perfect granddad is unafraid of big dogs
and fierce storms but absolutely terrified of the word 'boo.'
-Robert Brault

Scared Sheetless

December 2014

Everyone remembers Linus, right? He was Lucy's little brother in the *Peanuts* comic strip; the boy with his right thumb in his mouth and his left hand holding onto a security blanket for dear life. Time out for a quick comic strip history lesson: In the early days of *Peanuts*, a friend advised Linus that other children would tease him for having a security blanket. Linus responded by using his blanket as a whip to forcefully shear off the branch of a tree and said 'they never tease me more than once.'

That being said, my grandson Krischan reminds me of Linus. Krischan's right thumb will occasionally find its way to his mouth, he has his own version of a security blanket—a sheet passed down to him from his mother who used it when she was a child—and I doubt anyone would tease him more than once. The kid is absolutely fearless, and as far as I can tell he gets his courage from that piece of faded green and yellow cloth approximately the size of a twin-sized bed. Krischan finds strength from that sheet the way Samson found strength from his hair.

Beyond it being a source of security and courage, I've noticed Krischan uses the sheet for a number of other purposes, such as:

- A blanket. Krischan sleeps with his sheet every night and by the time he wakes up the next morning it looks like he's been swallowed up by a giant cocoon; a giant, faded green and yellow cloth cocoon.

- A tent. Krischan will drape the sheet over three or four chairs and voila: Instant fortress of Solitude. That clears the path for what every five-year old needs: Lots and lots of 'me time.'

- A cloak of invisibility. I notice Krischan uses it for this purpose quite often when he doesn't want to be disturbed—for instance, when he's watching *Scooby-Doo* cartoons—or when he's not ready to take a much-needed bath and decides to disappear. It works pretty well, at least up until the point he gives himself away by uncontrollably giggling… probably because he's amazed that he really has become invisible.

- A shield. When we're out in the woods hunting zombies and space aliens armed with only our plastic swords, Krischan will occasionally bring his impenetrable sheet with him. Just in case. Up until now the plastic swords have served us well, but there's always that first time that we'll need more than our swords and he wants to be ready.

I'll be honest: I've used the sheet once or twice myself:

- One time I heard Krischan making the sounds that I distinctly remember from when our two sons were his age: The sounds immediately preceding voracious projectile vomiting. Instinctively I grabbed his sheet, folded it over three or four times and held it in my hands like a gigantic catcher's mitt. *Steee-rike!* One flush of the toilet and one wash & dry cycle later and the sheet was good as new. Well, as new as a twenty-something year old sheet with an inherent musty smell about it can be, I guess.

- Another time Krischan got out of the tub and there wasn't a towel to be found. I spotted the sheet lying next to his pile of clothes by the side of the tub and wrapped Krischan up inside of it so at least some of the bath water could be absorbed. It was pretty obvious from all that nasty screaming that he could tell the difference between drying off with a soft, fluffy blanket and a thin, water repellant piece of faded green and yellow cloth.

I've tried my best to separate my grandson and his sheet but have yet to see signs of any real progress. I'm almost to the point of the 'if you can't beat em, join 'em' mindset.

That being said I'm sitting here in front of my keyboard with Krischan's faded green and yellow sheet draped across my lap. Maybe the kid has it all figured out: My legs are staying quite warm, I have projectile vomit insurance and I haven't seen the first sign of any zombies or space aliens.

I sheet you not.

**'In the eyes of children we find the joy of Christmas.
In their hearts we find its meaning.'**
-Leland Thomas

Catching that Holiday Spirit

December 2014

It was the first Friday night in December and the two of us were glued to the couch watching the Christmas double feature that every grandfather and grandson must watch together at some point: *A Christmas Carol* and *How the Grinch Stole Christmas*. Not the originals, mind you, but the modernized versions featuring the affable Jim Carrey. I'll admit it was the first time seeing either one of them for yours truly, but I could tell by Krischan's facial expressions that this certainly wasn't his first trip to Whoville or peek inside the mind of Ebenezer Scrooge.

Saturday morning came early. A bit chilly with occasional rain showers did nothing to dampen the enthusiasm of the young runner as he put on his running shoes—complete with jingle bells attached to the laces—to run the Jingle Bell Trail One-Mile Run. Prior to the start of the race Santa Claus, who would soon be giving the command to start the race, was standing directly in front of Krischan and I. I asked my grandson if he wanted me to take a picture of him with Santa… and he lightly punched me in the arm. If you have a grandson you may be familiar with this explanation of what was going on inside his mind at that very moment:

*Oh boy oh boy oh boy it's Santa Claus and he's
right next to me and I'm so excited
I can barely stand it but I have to play it cool and act like it's
no big thing because people are watching but oh boy oh boy it's
Santa and what can I do to disguise how excited I am
oh I know I'll punch my G-Pa in the arm because everyone will think
I'm laid back and much too cool for Santa and
they'll never know how excited I am that*

SANTA CLAUS IS RIGHT NEXT TO ME!!!

I'm guessing there were quite a few of you that had that last sentence in your head before you even read it. Verbatim, if I'm not mistaken.

As the two of us took our positions at the starting line I told Krischan to keep his eyes straight ahead since there were a lot of children in the race and I didn't want him to trip and fall. I said I would be directly behind him and instructed him not to look back for any reason. So what did he do for the first quarter-mile? He looked back every two or three seconds. I'm not sure if it was to make sure I was still with him or to make sure he was still beating me, but he did it A LOT and I know he could have run the race a little bit faster if he had kept his eyes straight ahead. In spite of everything—the looks back, the rain, the congestion caused by several hundred children running with jingle bells attached to their shoes—he beat his best time in the mile by over a minute.

Time to celebrate. We headed to the local frozen yogurt shop where Krischan asked me to fix him 'lots of choklit.' Chocolate frozen yogurt, chocolate sprinkles, chocolate chips, chocolate syrup and a scoop of gummi spiders (don't ask): *Let the celebration begin!*

We headed home as we still had about 90 minutes to kill before the second part of our day was about to start. I used the time to recover; Krischan used the time to reload.

Before I knew what hit me we headed out for the annual Light Up Senoia (LUS) festivities. We arrived several hours before the event would begin; you know, to make sure we would get 'a good seat.' (Later on it was clear that had we arrived at one-minute-to-LUS we would have had the exact same 'seat.') So after killing a couple of hours visiting The Walking Dead store, eating a chocolate (is there any other flavor?) pudding in The Walking Dead Café, visiting The Walking Dead Museum, taking in a few of *The Walking Dead* sites in town and spending a good 30 minutes hunting a few of The Walking Dead on our own (Krischan came prepared:

Zombie Nerf gun was firmly in hand at all times) it was time for the show to go on.

But first we had to get a large bag of hand-spun cotton candy that soon turned Krischan's hands and face completely blue. After a visit to the local pizza parlor for a 'cleanup in aisle three,' we took our spot in the center of town to watch the launch of LUS.

Two local radio 'celebrities' (they host a car show on the local country music station) introduced the homegrown talent. Baton twirlers were followed by fiddlers were followed by (OK, time to fess up: I have no idea who the third performers were because this was when we actually were at the pizza parlor trying to de-blue Krischan)…

At this point there were still 20 minutes until the parade would start. So we head down to the Senoia Masonic Lodge because, after all, Krischan's face wasn't going to paint itself!

It was there we waited about 15 minutes for our appointment with Dusty the Clown. Three minutes (and $5) later Krischan sported the cutest reindeer face you'd ever hope to find on a boy too cool for Santa. If I'm not mistaken he looked like one of the characters I saw in Whoville the night before. *(Kudos, Dusty!)*

Five minutes later we had front-row spots along the parade route. I made a mental note not to show up three hours before the parade in the future, while my grandson and his little reindeer smile giggled in anticipation of seeing his very first parade… and of course Santa Claus.

Having never been to a parade in a small town I didn't know what to expect, but it didn't take long to see the pattern: Baton twirlers who we'd seen earlier when they were performing in one spot but not marching as they were now, members of a local church (with a 'float'—actually a trailer with a manger and a faux Jesus and faux Mary cradling a baby doll), local merchant handing out candy to the children, local Boy Scout troop, two of the Budweiser Clydesdales (we saw them earlier but I didn't mention them because they sort of frightened Krischan, the same boy who has no problem fighting flesh-eating zombies), local marching band, classic car, local church handing out candy to the children, local merchant, local marching band handing out candy to the children, classic car, local Girl Scout troop, people on horseback (Horse #3: PLOP! Children along parade route: EWWWW!!! Note: Carrying large pail behind horses in a parade is the second worst job in the world. The worst job in the world? Carrying a large shovel behind horses in a parade.) and more candy candy candy candy candy... and then... AND THEN...

Santa *AND* Mrs. Claus!

It was then I saw the smile I had hoped for nine hours earlier when Krischan was standing a foot away from the Man in Red. The smile of a young boy filled with hopes and dreams. The smile of a young boy who doesn't yet understand the meaning of peace on earth and good will towards man, but give him time. The smile of a young boy who throughout the afternoon gave a generous amount of his candy to the little girl standing beside him along the parade route because she was having trouble getting it on her own. The smile of a young boy, simply reminding you that there is nothing *like* the smile of a young boy.

As I remember our day together I realize I won't have any trouble this year getting my fair share of the Christmas spirit.

The kid's got enough for the both of us.

On the seventh day God rested. His grandchildren
must have been out of town.
- Gene Perret

Skarlette

December 2014

Krischan went ice-skating with his Uncle Josh a couple nights ago. I wasn't there, but thanks to a 30-clip of video Josh captured on his cell phone I was able to see how my grandson handled skating on thin ice for the first time in his life. Three words: Not very well.

You've seen the cartoons where the rabbit, the cat or the mouse—in an attempt to escape the jaws of death from a larger adversary—begins pumping its legs in a circular motion for several seconds before the legs take hold and they actually begin running, right? It was just like that, except Krischan was holding onto the side rail for dear life while his skates were digging a six-inch crevice in the ice. While it lacked in grace, it sure was fun to watch.

But I'm not here to discuss Krischan's outlook for the Winter Olympic Games a decade or so down the road. Rather, this is about Krischan's new friend Skarlette.

Beautiful long reddish-brown hair, dangling earrings and an infectious gap-toothed smile that melts your heart, Skarlette is the daughter of Josh's lovely girlfriend Bernice. Only eight years old, Skarlette already has the quiet wisdom and insight of a young lady well beyond her years. She is also—and this may be one of the reasons Krischan took to her so quickly—one of the boys.

Skarlette came to visit us during the Christmas holidays and as Krischan does with all first-timers who come to our new home in Senoia, he wanted to take them out on the trail in the woods behind the house to hunt zombies. First things first: Weapons. I grabbed my foam sword in the garage and Krischan grabbed his, leaving the plastic sword that nobody uses because the blade breaks every time you hit a tree limb with it for Skarlette. To her credit, she didn't complain one bit.

She fell in line behind the Captain of the mission (Krischan) and his soldier (me) as we began blazing the trail behind the house. Following Krischan's lead, Skarlette began swinging her sword at every branch, vine and plant that she encountered. She was a natural.

At one point I stopped to pick up a stick and threw it about 10 feet in front of Krischan (I do this all the time when we're in the woods and almost every time he doesn't know I threw it). Krischan raised his arms (as he always does when he doesn't know I threw the stick) and said *'nobody move, I heard a clue.'* I looked back at Skarlette and she had both hands over her mouth, fighting back a giggle that I'm certain would have sounded like a melody had it been audible. About a minute later Skarlette bent over to pick up a stick and did the exact same thing I had done earlier, and it had the same results. *'Nobody move, I heard a clue.'* I looked over at Skarlette and she had her hands clamped down on her mouth so tight I thought her big brown eyes were going to pop out of her tiny head.

The rest of the weekend Krischan and Skarlette were inseparable. They sat next to one another on the couch for quite a while Saturday night; Krischan was mesmerized by Skarlette's prowess playing the latest video games. I might add that it was obvious Krischan is in no hurry to impress the ladies: he sat close to Skarlette the entire time, looking over her shoulder with his security sheet firmly in hand and his thumb in his mouth. In fact the only words he said over a two-hour window of time was when he asked for ice water because his *'breath was hot.'* Charming, eh Skarlette?

Sunday morning we all went to church (Krischan loves church— *'they have a playground'*). He insisted Skarlette come to his classroom, full of kindergarten age children a couple of years younger than her.

Skarlette wouldn't have had it any other way: The two of them were inseparable during this special, memorable weekend.

It was pure magic.

My grandchild has taught me what true love means.
It means watching Scooby-Doo cartoons while the
basketball game is on the other channel.
-Gene Perret

Doctor's Orders

December 2014

Christmas was over, the New Year was approaching and I had six days off from work to spend with Krischan and relax. Well, that plan worked for a couple of days up until the point that whatever it was that had been keeping Krischan under the weather had found its way over to me. That's when the fun began.

Let me explain how this particular 'fun' worked. A persistent cough that felt like a scalding hot, razor sharp blade was penetrating my chest cavity. Sneezes were similar although more painful; much more so, in fact. Congestion that couldn't have been any worse if a vise was holding my nostrils closed. Constant chills, except for the occasional times when I became so hot my clothes became soaked in perspiration in a matter of seconds; an overall weakness that defied any and all logic and that skin-hurting-when-clothing-touches-it thingee that probably never will be explained if we all live for a thousand years.

And lest I forget, what 'fun' wouldn't be complete without a total loss of appetite and a perpetual desire for nothing other than restful, healing, pretend-it-don't-hurt-no-more sleep?

So now that you understand my definition of 'fun,' know those last four days of my vacation time with Krischan were exactly as I described and for those reasons I will always remember them as fun. The kind of fun you'll always hold dear in your memory.

Because for those four days Krischan did everything he could to 'take care of his G-Pa.' For those 96 hours he was the embodiment of every flawless albeit fictional doctor I watched on television while I was growing up.

Don't believe me? Get out your scorecard and you'll see how well young Marcus Welby MD fared:

Compassion: With every cough (or sneeze) as I lay prone on the couch, Krischan would lean over and kiss me on the cheek to make me feel better. The crazy thing is it worked every time, because I actually *did* feel better.

Medical care: At regular intervals (it seemed like every two hours, but I was in-and-out most of the time so it's hard to gauge exactly) Krischan told me it was time for my medicine. He would then give me one piece of raspberry sorbet Ice Breaker's Ice Cubes chewing gum and then help himself to one as well because it was not only medicine but 'our favorite gum' as well.

Proper treatment: As Krischan patiently* sat by me on the couch as 'just a few more minutes' turned into hours that turned into several hours after that, he would reach over and rub my forehead, neck or shoulders. (*Patience to a five-year old constitutes having a fully-charged iPad on one's lap and the Nicktoons channel playing on the television. Now you know.)

Patience: As previously described and to include other ways of passing the time. Like drawing one's own bath, for instance. Krischan asked if he could take a bath (he had a plastic alligator and four frogs he wanted to play with in the tub). I asked if he was able to take a bath without me, and the next thing I knew I heard the bath water running. An hour (two?) later I called out to see if he was ready to get out of the tub. 'Not yet.' An hour (two?) after that I asked again and got the same answer. This time I wasn't taking no for an answer (translation: I was now able to pry myself off the couch) so I went into the bathroom and found Krischan splashing around in no more than three inches of very cool bath water... without any evidence any actual bathing had occurred. I ran some warm water and poured a cup of it on his head so I could wash his hair. The next thing I know he's screaming 'it's hot—it's hot.' It was barely lukewarm, but I guess when you've been sitting in cool bath water for two (four?) hours or so it would give the illusion of being hot. All this to say: Krischan did a good job occupying his time while I was sleeping. I'm just grateful he didn't turn into a prune.

Accountability: Not once during those four days did more than a few hours go by before Krischan would touch his palm to my forehead and offer his medical opinion of my current condition. 'Yep, you still have a temp-a-toor' seemed to be the most popular one offered. (I believe it was fairly accurate.)

I'm not sure I would have made it through those four days without him: Cindy was working, I didn't feel like doing a single, solitary thing and I'm a man and you know how needie we are when we're sick.

Having Krischan watch over me those four days was just what the doctor ordered.

Me, G-Pa, Yia-Yia and the Gnome

When grandparents enter the door, discipline flies out the window.
-Ogden Nash

Barter System

January 2015

'G-Pa, hold out your hand. I've got a sur-PRIZE for you.'

That can only mean one thing. Krischan is about to place a Hot Tamale—or as he calls it a 'hot kamale'—in my hand. If you're not familiar with Hot Tamales, think of them as cinnamon-flavored Mike and Ike's and know that they are a favorite of Krischan and I. Now understand that a Hot Tamale held tightly in a human hand for anything more than a few seconds causes it to begin melting, so by the time the 'surprise' is in my hand it's warm, gooey and turns the palm of my hand bright red. Then again, it's one of my favorites so I normally eat it without any fuss.

But this time I noticed Krischan didn't have any Hot Tamales in his other hand for himself. He also didn't stick around to watch me eat the Hot Tamale; instead he wandered off into the kitchen. I heard him going into the kitchen pantry where all of the candy in the house is stored. I gave him a minute or so before checking on him and found him on the couch—opening five pieces of my absolute favorite candy, something Krischan is well aware of---Kraft Caramels. Judging by the clandestine manner in which he snuck off into the kitchen once I had my Hot Tamale in hand, the caramels were apparently now his absolute favorite candy as well. I found it intriguing how he 'bought me off' with a Hot Tamale and went after the caramels for himself.

But it didn't surprise me. The boy has shown me time and time again what a clever and calculating mind he has. You can practically see a frantic mouse running on the wheel inside his head when he's thinking (unless he's watching television or playing on the iPad because then it's pretty clear the wheel is abandoned). Over the years I've learned to cope, compensate and circumvent some of Krischan's more—I'll say this as gently as I can— 'undesirable' behaviors.

For example there are several things nearly impossible to get him to do if he's not on the same page. For example:

- If I want him to take a bath because he's beginning to smell like the wet towel I left in my gym locker in 11th grade, I'll have to offer something up. What I've found works best is taking him with me to the grocery store and letting him get one of the $1 rubber animals (his favorites include sharks, dolphins, dinosaurs and giant bugs). That way I can use the animal later as incentive to take a bath because he LOVES to play in the tub with his toys—especially the new ones because that way he can introduce everyone to one another.

- If I want him to play outside (when the television and/or iPad is the reason he wants to stay inside because otherwise he LOVES being outside) I'll have to convince him I've seen 'something moving' in the woods behind the house and that it needs our attention *immediately*. It's not long before we both have our foam rubber swords in hand and are heading out towards the trees so we can keep the residents of the subdivision safe. Of course buying him a new foam rubber sword seems to work quite well also.

- If I want him to play inside (when there's inclement weather, when I'm exhausted because he and I spent the entire day in the woods hunting moving things) I'll have to sweeten the deal by offering him chocolate milk, blueberries or Kraft caramels (formerly Hot Tamales). Offering to watch an animated movie seems to work, too (favorites include *Despicable Me*, *Wreck It Ralph* and all of the different flavors of *Madagascar*).

- If I need to run an errand in the car and Krischan doesn't want to go, I have found there's a good chance he'll change his mind if I promise to drive by an old house I saw that appears to be haunted, stop to feed carrots or apples to the horses along the highway or go to McDonald's for a Happy Meal.

As for the trip to McDonald's, it's not really the Happy Meal he's after. It's the toy inside. That and the in-restaurant playground.

For a REAL challenge, try and get Krischan to leave a McDonald's playground. You know, the ones with the bouncy cage that smell like that wet towel I mentioned earlier. It's virtually impossible.

Even if you offered him all the Kraft caramels he can eat.

A child can ask questions that a wise man cannot answer.
-Author Unknown

Getting Schooled

January 2015

Krischan has been undergoing a growth spurt recently. I'm not talking about getting taller—although he has grown two inches in the past three months—but rather I'm talking about his mind. The boy has become a wealth of information. It makes me wonder what I missed by never going to kindergarten when I was his age.

Krischan spent the weekend with Cindy and I. Here's an abbreviated list of what he taught me in a whirlwind day-and-a-half catching me up on what I missed out on:

- 'A Kawana bear lives in the jungles of Australia. It's a bear but doesn't look like a bear. Weird, huh?'

- 'Daddy Longlegs aren't really spiders. They're just disguised as spiders so they can protect humans from real spiders.'

- 'Music makes the characters come to life, like in *Peter and the Wolf.* Do you know Peter and the Wolf. The wolf ate a duck but threw it back up. Do you know that a black duck is poisonous? That's because it brushed up against a poisonous plant and it turned its fur black and made it that way. Don't touch a black duck.'

- 'A bear is a carnivore because it eats meat. Humans are horvivores because we eat healthy. Stuff like fruits and vegetables. And meat.'

- 'Mama bears hold their baby bears on their chest so the baby can hear its mama's heartbeat. That's the mama bear's way of telling her baby she loves it.'

- 'It's OK to touch poison ivy with your hands because you have special skin on your hand; sort of like a snake. But if you touch your face after holding poison ivy your face will become poisonous.'

- 'If you cut an 8 in half you end up with a 3. If you turn a 5 upside down you have a 2.'

- 'It's really hot on the sun. That's because there are a lot of volcanoes with hot lava coming out of them. The biggest volcano is called the Pile of Doom.'

- 'Red ants bite and it hurts and stings like fire. Black ants bite but it only hurts. That's because they don't have fire in them like red ants do.'

- 'In the '80's they called penguins fish with arms.'

- 'Hanitizer' is Krischan's syllable-saving and more logical word for 'hand sanitizer.'

Krischan had so much to tell me I had to take notes. Apparently I missed out on quite a lot when I was a boy.

But I'm catching up fast.

Grandparents are there to help the child get into
mischief they haven't thought of yet.
—Gene Perret

Man Date

January 2015

I got back from my Saturday morning run and Krischan was already sitting on the couch, engrossed in one of the latest video games that is so above my pay grade I couldn't tell you what it was or how it was played if my life depended on it. I asked him if he wanted me to fix him the usual for breakfast (frozen waffles) only to find out his Yia-Yia already made them for him. I remember the last time Cindy made him waffles he wouldn't eat them because they weren't 'crunchy like G-Pa's.' I asked Krischan what changed and he told me he 'showed her how to make them.' Apparently there's more than one way to turn a toaster oven on.

We had the whole day in front of us with nothing official on our agendas, freeing us up to do what Krischan refers to as 'man things.' We started the day by running a couple of errands that resulted in a couple gallons of ice cream we didn't really need and a large bag of gummi candy that would be ancient history well before lunchtime Sunday. We came home and had lunch: Spicy chicken sandwiches and veggie straws. Let me be the first to say, if there's a five-year old on the planet who likes vegetables more than Krischan then he must be a rabbit. He looked at the veggie straws, held up a red one and said 'ooh, this one is tomato!' Then he asked if he could have a real tomato while pushing the chicken sandwich ('it's too spicy!') to the side.

After lunch we went down to the basement to assemble a weight bench we will be using in the months ahead to 'make our muscles bigger.' While I removed what must have been 1,000 pieces out of the 2' X 4' cardboard box, Krischan picked up Cindy's five-pound hand barbells and proceeded to flaunt his muscles while I was trying to distinguish those

1,000 different parts that the directions referred to by part number but apparently the manufacturer didn't think it important to indicate these part numbers on the parts themselves. It's a good thing I had my trusty assistant to help, because it was a lot easier having Krischan bring me the 15 or so parts that MIGHT be 'Part # 127' than it was for me to get up from my seat each time to siphon through the parts until I found the right one.

The entire construction process took the two of us about four hours. All I had to show for that time was a sore back from bending over, a sore right arm from tightening about 500 screws and twice that many bolts and a patience that was on the verge of detonating. Oh yeah: And a really great weight bench that in all honesty will never give me a workout nearly as strenuous as the one it gave me today while assembling it. As for Krischan, he discovered the batteries in his remote-control motorcycle still had life, that a lot of my Florida Gator memorabilia doubled as playthings (he walked around all afternoon wearing my authentic leather football helmet) and that his G-Pa could build really big things all by himself (at which point I reminded him that I couldn't have done it without his help).

We then retired to the couch and turned on the Florida-Arkansas basketball game. Krischan noticed the Florida Gator logo in the middle of the court and said 'everyone likes the Gators' and noticed that the fans on television were all cheering for them. He said 'I like the Gators' before telling me that 'the Gators have 43 and the Hogs have 37.' This surprised me on several levels: (1) I didn't know he could read double-digit numbers, (2) I never told him the opposing team was the Hogs and (3) I didn't know how he could distinguish which team had which number of points so I asked him about all three. In order: (1) 'G-Pa, I can count to one hundred!' (2) 'They have hogs on their uniforms and the Gators will win because gators eat hogs.' (3) 'I know you've tried to teach Yia-Yia that when the teams are listed on the screen side-by-side the home team is on the right and when the teams are listed one on top of the other the home team is on the bottom, and today the Gators were listed on the right.' (I totally made that last one up but in the hopes that Cindy will read this one day maybe it will sink in once and for all.)

Florida ended up winning the game (gators eat hogs, remember?) and Krischan summed it up best when he said:

'That was the best football game I've ever seen.'

The goose over my right shoulder hissed at me!

Surely, two of the most satisfying experiences in life must be those of being a grandchild or a grandparent.
– Donald A. Norberg

New Kid in Hogtown

February 2015

Returning to Gainesville, Florida for a visit is one of Cindy and my favorite things to do. For one reason it's where we went to college and it's always fun to take in the sights—those that have been in existence since we were enrolled as well as those that came on the scene well after we graduated many years ago. For another it allows us to engage in one of our favorite activities: 'Gator shopping.' I know the local businesses have appreciated our loyal and generous support over the years. I can tell because all of them send us Christmas cards.

Another reason is that occasionally we have the opportunity to show off our favorite city to someone else for the very first time. Our most recent trip to Gainesville was no exception, because that was when we formally introduced Krischan to the magic of the home of the Florida Gators, also known as 'Hogtown' by the locals and the student body.

We made the five-hour drive from Senoia to Gainesville on a Saturday. That evening we had dinner at the home of friends of ours (also Gators, of course) who just so happen to have a three-year old son. Krischan was a natural playing 'big brother' to his new friend and when it came time to head to our hotel it was all we could do to convince him it was time to go.

'Yes, Krischan we know it's early but G-Pa has a marathon to run in the morning and he'd like to get at least a couple hours of sleep before he has to run 26 miles.'

Cindy tried her best. Only this is apparently what Krischan actually heard her say:

'G-Pa said we need to leave NOW and yes I know you're having a great time playing with the train set and watching cartoons with your friend but your G-Pa is pure evil and wants nothing more than to make your life miserable.'

Well, at least I'd be getting a couple hours of sleep before running 26 miles.

Race morning I asked Cindy to take Krischan and meet me at a specific spot on the course so he could run the final quarter-mile with me, thus allowing the two of us to cross the finish line together (I had already cleared this ahead of time with the Race Director). With almost 26 miles under my belt I met up with Krischan, and he immediately started running so fast it was as if it was his way of punishing me for making his life miserable the night before.

As we neared the finish line I slowed down slightly so Krischan could cross the finish line a step in front of me. I made eye contact with a volunteer and motioned for her to place the finisher's medal around Krischan's neck and she politely obliged. The smile on his face was… well, let's just say that 'miserable' was no longer in either one of our vocabularies.

(A little background: Krischan has completed four one-mile fun runs. All of these fun runs had an accompaning 5-kilometer (3.1 miles) race. Krischan, upon completing his fun runs invariably asks me if he will be getting a medal. I always give him the same answer: Medals are only given for the longer race. The stage is now set for the next paragraph.)

Krischan's beaming smile was momentarily interrupted by this rather insightful comment:

'Gee, that didn't FEEL like three miles!'

After a couple slices of post-race pizza we headed back to the hotel for a short nap and a shower. We then headed out to stimulate the local economy and did our very best to buy every new product in orange and blue the city had to offer (Note: We were $ucce$$ful).

Our new favorite store selling 'all things Gator' is called Alumni Hall. Let me tell you: It was literally the kid in the candy store. Krischan seemed to like it, too. Wearing his new orange Gator T-shirt, Krischan made a point to do the 'Gator Chomp' for one of the girls ringing up one of our purchases while making it perfectly clear he doesn't like the Bulldogs (of the University of Georgia). I doubt it's possible for any grandfather to have been any prouder of their grandson than I was of mine at that particular moment in time.

We then turned our attention to taking Krischan to see some of the places on campus that make the University of Florida so special. Our first stop was Ben Hill Griffin Stadium and Florida Field, also known as 'the Swamp.' How did he enjoy his first trip inside the house that Tim Tebow, Emmitt Smith and Steve Spurrier built? Let me answer with a simple equation:

$$\text{Excited boy} + \text{empty 88,548 seats} + \text{an unscripted Sunday afternoon} = \text{88,548 possible places to sit}$$

I should have remembered that from my freshman calculus class and probably would have… had I not taken the class over 40 years ago. And studied.

Outside the stadium we stopped to see the bronze statues of the three Gator Heisman Trophy winners; Tebow, Spurrier and Danny Wuerffel. I asked Krischan to sit in front of the latter's statue so I could take a photograph, reminding him that he had met Danny Wuerffel several months ago at the College Football Hall of Fame. You may remember that Krischan wasn't too impressed meeting the quarterback of Florida's first National Championship football team in person. Well, let me be the first to tell you Krischan was even *less* impressed with his bronze statue.

Getting him to sit still for a single picture was slightly less difficult than getting him to leave our friends' house the night before.

However, he *was* impressed with the bronze statue of an alligator sitting outside the stadium. He was even more impressed with he saw a second bronzed alligator twice the size of the first. In fact he asked me to take pictures of him in a variety of positions: With his arm stuck inside the alligator's mouth, riding the alligator bareback and lying beneath it as if he was in the midst of an alligator stampede (should there be such a thing). It was nothing less than Reptile Heaven for a wide-eyed five-year old boy getting his introduction to the mystique of the Swamp.

With a little time left to kill before joining our friends for dinner, we made quick stops at the O'Connell Center (the 'O-Dome'), where the Gator basketball team plays home games and Lake Alice, one of the favorite spots for student recreation (alas, there were no live alligators to be seen, although there were white heron everywhere).

Krischan seemed to really enjoy his orange and blue weekend. So much, in fact that once we got back home I wrote 'Florida' between the words 'Krischan' and 'Kollege Fund' on the envelope that won't be needed for another 12 years.

Twelve years that will most certainly go by in the blink of an eye.

Or as quick as a Gator Chomp.

I want one of these!

Elephants and grandchildren never forget.
-Andy Rooney

Family Circus

March 2015

Krischan was so excited this morning because today was the day he was GOING TO THE CIRCUS!

After all, this was in all likelihood the last item on whatever a young boy would call a list of things he wanted to do before he started first grade. A bucket list for preschoolers, perhaps.

All of the other items on the list had been checked off:

- First haircut.

- First birthday party, as well as…

- First attempt at finishing off an entire chocolate cake in one sitting.

- First trip to the movie theater (*The Lorax*, if you must know).

- First trip to the emergency room (no cause for alarm; he was fine).

- First trip to the zoo.

- First day of kindergarten.

- First friend who was a girl but by no means did that make her his girlfriend.

- First trip to the aquarium.

- First trip to the University of Florida (OK, so taking my grandson may have been on *my* bucket list).

- First trip to the College Football Hall of Fame (maybe this one as well).

- First pair of running shoes (last one from me. Promise.).

- First visit from the Tooth Fairy.

So all that remained on the list was a trip to the circus. And what did the trip to the circus mean to a starry-eyed young boy a few weeks shy of his sixth birthday? ELEPHANTS! THE STRONG MAN! ELEPHANTS! CLOWNS! ELEPHANTS! LIONS! TIGERS!

And MORE ELEPHANTS!

When we arrived at the Gwinnett Arena I asked Krischan if there would be any dragons in the circus. *'No, G-Pa; dragons aren't real.'* Roger that.

Once we were inside the arena Krischan immediately asked if he could get a box of popcorn to eat during the show. As it was dinnertime and we hadn't eaten since lunchtime I took out my wallet, only to discover a box of popcorn would require me to take out a 15-year loan. I noticed that cotton candy required a 30-year loan, but it did come with a free quasi-Ringmaster hat so I convinced Krischan he really wanted the cotton candy that in all probability was closer to the truth anyway.

Once we found our seats, you'll never guess the first word out of his mouth when the Ringmaster announced the beginning of 'the greatest show on earth.' *'DRAGONS!!!'* as he stood and pointed at the two costumed dragons leading the procession of circus performers onto the arena floor. I bit my tongue so hard I'm pretty sure it bled a little.

Once the performance began, Krischan was mesmerized. There were clowns and ELEPHANTS and motorcycles and ELEPHANTS and trapeze artists and ELEPHANTS and gymnasts and ELEPHANTS and lions, tigers and ELEPHANTS.

But alas, there was no strong man. Not until intermission, that is. Because that was when Krischan demonstrated that *he* was the strong man by challenging me to an endless series of arm-wrestling competitions he had no trouble winning because the palms of his hands were coated in pink and baby blue cotton candy and not only that were kind of sweaty and I just wanted the whole thing to be over with because now MY hands were becoming pink, baby blue and very, very sticky.

Throughout the first half of the show Krischan mentioned he wanted a circus sword, a three-foot piece of plastic that glowed in the dark… and cost approximately the price of admission to the show.

Krischan: *I want a sword.*

Me: *You already have a circus hat.*

Krischan: *I want a sword.*

Me: *AND you have cotton candy.*

Krischan: *I want a sword.*

Me: *AND you're getting to enjoy 'the greatest show on earth.'*

Krischan: *I. Want. A. Sword.*

I mentioned intermission earlier. Intermission was actually a time the circus owners intended for you to take your children to the lobby and spend your life's earnings on stuffed animals, plastic toys and other circus paraphernalia that will most likely end up in next spring's garage sale. Now you know why I chose pink, baby blue and very, very sticky hands as my intermission option.

An announcement was made: *'Three minutes until the show resumes. Everyone take your seats.'*

'If I can just make it for another 180 seconds I just might dodge the sword bullet...'

That was the thought in my head as a vendor with his arms full of plastic swords ran up the stairs and stopped right next to where I was sitting (I'm just lucky that way).

'Sword! Sword! Sword! Sword! Sword!'

That would have been fine had those words come out of the mouth of the vendor. However, they were coming out of the mouth of the little boy sitting next to me who should have been wearing his ringmaster hat but instead was desperate to hold one of those precious swords in his sticky little hands.

I started counting in my head. *'One Mississippi... two Mississippi...'*

Thankfully the lights soon dimmed, the show resumed and Krischan's attention returned to the center ring where it stayed until the very last clown left the arena.

As we left the arena I did my very best to avoid anyone with a glow-in-the-dark sword in their hand. It was no problem spotting them, because it was basically everyone except us.

Postcript: I couldn't decide if seeing the Harlem Globetrotters should be included on Krischan's list of things to do before elementary school. So I asked him to watch a video clip of the Globetrotters in action to judge his reaction. One of the Globetrotters was sitting on the rim and the referee ran towards him, yelling at him to 'get down!' Kool and the Gang's *Jungle Boogie* came blaring over the sound system. The Globetrotter stood up on the rim and began shaking his moneymaker, doing his best to 'get down.' I thought it was hilarious. Krischan was nowhere to be found.

For the time being I'm putting the Harlem Globetrotters on the back burner.

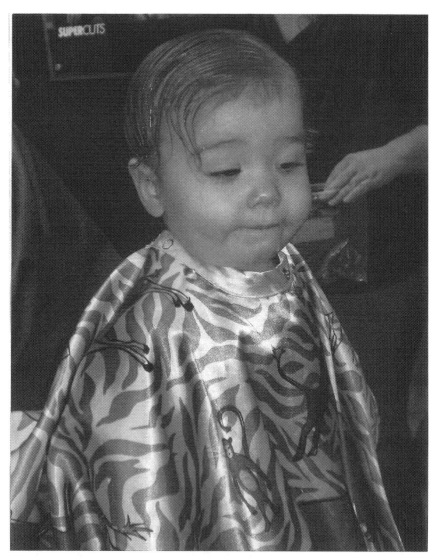

My first haircut; can you tell?

Cleaning your house while your kids are still growing up
is like shoveling the walk before it stops snowing.
-Phyllis Diller

Country Mile

March 2015

There are plenty of reasons Cindy and I decided to move to the country last year. Tranquility, peace and quiet and starry, starry nights are just the tips of the iceberg we now call home: Senoia, Georgia.

It's no secret that the beautiful and scenic country roads had quite the influence on me as well. Words can't express how much I love running on wide open, rolling asphalt roads weaving through the pastures, woods and lakes in the still of a quiet and lazy morning in the country.

It's also no secret (to most, anyway) that Senoia, Georgia is also home of the hit television show *The Walking Dead*. I first started running in Senoia several years ago; it was the spring of 2012, to be exact. I had always heard how beautiful the area was and I wanted to see for myself… with one goal in mind: If it was as beautiful as I was led to believe I wanted to establish a race—The Running Dead Ultra, it would be called—that meandered through Senoia and took in many of the sites used in the production of the show.

The first Running Dead Ultra was held on the country roads of Senoia the very next year. The year after that Cindy and I moved there.

The third Running Dead Ultra will be held soon. As a way of giving back to the community, I thought it might be appropriate to spend some time picking up trash along the sides of one of the roads on which the race would be held. I selected one of my personal favorites, Dead Oak. Fans of *The Walking Dead* might recognize Dead Oak as the road many of the 'driving-in-the-car scenes' are filmed. I recognize it as my absolute favorite country road to run.

Last weekend I asked my grandson if he wanted to spend some time picking up trash with me when he visited the following weekend. He didn't hesitate: *Yes!* I wouldn't have expected anything less from a boy who loves being at Cindy's store (he has a knack for charming his customers; yes, *his* customers) and spending time with me at my 'workhouse' (he has a knack for eating the sweets my admin gives him).

So this fine Saturday morning I asked Krischan if he remembered what we would be doing today. He certainly did: *'We're picking up trash on the side of the road. Can we go to McDonald's when we're finished?'* The question you can't say 'no' to, right?

So I grabbed a couple of large black plastic trash bags, Krischan grabbed his plastic knife and gun to fight any zombies we might run into and we hopped in the truck and headed over to Dead Oak Road.

We spent the next couple of hours picking up every piece of trash we could find along a one-mile stretch of country road. Well, actually Krischan did the picking while I held the bag. Krischan was a real trooper, making sure he got every single beer bottle, paper cup and potato chip bag he ran across into our large black plastic bag.

And I use the word 'ran' in the literal sense: If I didn't know better I would have sworn Krischan was on an Easter egg hunt. In his mind every piece of trash was pure gold. He was running up embankments to get his hands on a plastic cup lid, then sliding back down on his fanny after losing his footing on the slippery pine needles. He was throwing caution to the wind reaching into sharp, prickly vegetation to get his hands on a candy bar wrapper. He was—after looking both ways for oncoming traffic, of course (we only saw one car all afternoon; more on that in a moment)—darting back and forth across the road, as he didn't want to miss inspecting everything and anything that wasn't green.

Every time we ran across two or three beer bottles or soda cans in close proximity Krischan said it looked like *'somebody had a party here.'* I asked him who would have a party on the side of the road. Without hesitation he replied: *'Party dudes.'* I looked at him and asked, *'Seriously, party dudes?'* Doubting himself and replying with more of a question than a statement, he said *'Party poopers?'*

This led to my explanation of what constituted a 'litter bug' and Krischan, never at a loss for questions asked who would do such a bad thing to nature. I asked him what he learned in kindergarten about nature. He replied: *'Nature is beautiful.'* I told him he was right, but every now and then nature needed a helping hand. That's where we came in.

Back to that one car we saw while we were picking up trash. An elderly woman was driving by and stopped once she came upon us. She asked if 'the blue truck a ways back' was ours. I told her it was. She told us how much she appreciated what Krischan and I were doing. I told her I appreciated her saying that while Krischan was busy diving into a ditch to retrieve an empty plastic gallon milk jug. I don't think I could have been prouder of my grandson than I was at that very moment. As I write these words the memory of that moment still warms my heart: The pride of being a grandparent, no doubt.

Once Krischan and I secured every single piece of garbage, trash and litter we could lay our eyes and Krischan could get his hands on, we threw it all in the back of our truck and headed east on Dead Oak for our much-deserved lunch. About two miles down the road we saw an elderly woman picking up trash that had brushed up against a fence along the side of the road. It was the same woman who had stopped to thank us earlier. I believe the woman lives on the horse farm the fence surrounds and that maybe picking up trash was something she does on a regular basis.

Then again, maybe she was simply inspired by a little boy three generations her junior.

Postscript: My friend Valerie and I ran on Dead Oak Road the very next morning. The one-mile stretch that Krischan and I spent our Saturday afternoon removing trash was noticeably more 'natural' than the rest of the road. With Krischan by my side, I hope to keep it that way.

I'm doing my part to keep Senoia clean!

*You can judge a man's true character by the
way he treats his fellow animals.*
— Paul McCartney

Puppy Love

March 2015

My friend Valerie introduced Ariel to a group of us the other day. It
was obvious Ariel wasn't comfortable around us, and with good reason:
Her previous owner had abandoned her only a week earlier. If it weren't for
Valerie finding her (Valerie owns the house in which Ariel was left behind
and inspected it a couple of days after it was vacated), who knows what
might have become of the innocent blue-eyed, golden-haired ball of fur
barely a couple of months old.

As Valerie held Ariel in her arms, I slowly extended my hand out to
Ariel's nose to allow her to do whatever it is dogs do to make sure it's safe
for a human to pet them. A muffled growl accompanied an expression that
can best be described as 'gee-I-really-really-want-to-be-petted-but-gosh-
darn-is-it-safe-I-mean-is-it-really-really-safe?' So after Ariel pulled away
once or twice she reluctantly let me pet her on the head for a few seconds,
before she started getting anxious and began growling a little bit louder
and a little bit longer than she had earlier. Realizing what Ariel had been
through over the last week, I couldn't blame her one bit.

Then the coolest thing happened. My son drove up and my grandson
Krischan—peering out the window and spotting the puppy in Valerie's
arms—jumped out of the car and ran towards Ariel as fast as his little legs
would carry him. Meanwhile Ariel did everything in her power to free
herself from Valerie's arms, wriggling back and forth as hard as she could
while whining hysterically--as all puppies do when they want something
and want it *now*. Valerie placed her on the ground and in the blink of an eye
Ariel was rolling over on her back in front of a kneeling Krischan, begging
for him to rub her stomach. From then on the two were inseparable until

the time we left. Ariel nipped at Krischan's limbs again and again, but according to him 'it didn't hurt.' Love nibbles, no doubt.

It was obvious Ariel had a problem trusting adults. After being abandoned—left alone in a house with no food or water—who could blame her? But when it came to this particular six-year old boy, Ariel knew she could trust him... that he would do her no harm. Animals have that sixth sense allowing them to discern good from evil... a warm heart from a cold heart... a friend from an enemy... someone whose heart was filled with love, compassion and innocence.

Animals just know.

Cindy and I have five cats in our household. All of them are of the 'lost and found' variety: They were lost and we found them. Maui, the elder statesman of the group is the sweetest cat you would ever want to meet. However, meeting him is another story. Outside of Cindy and I, Maui isn't too keen on being around people. But when it comes to Krischan, Maui jumps up on the couch beside him and holds one paw in the air, his polite way of asking to be petted. It was fairly obvious Maui knew Krischan would never do him any harm; that he is his friend.

Animals just know.

There is a house a couple miles from ours with two horses and a donkey inside of the large, fenced-in yard. Since Krischan had never seen a donkey before (other than the animated one in *Shrek*) we drove to the house so he could catch a glimpse. The owner of the property, seeing a little boy standing on his gate and peering into his yard, walked over and asked Krischan if he would like to see his animals. It doesn't take a rocket scientist to know what happened next.

Ginny the donkey was a lot like Maui: She didn't appear to have any interest in being around humans. Curious George, the larger of the two horses was another story. He couldn't stay away from Krischan. As Krischan carefully walked through the field, being particularly mindful not to step on any 'surprises,' Curious George followed right behind. Every couple of seconds Curious George nudged Krischan with his rather large head with enough force to push him a couple of feet to the side each time. But Krischan was more interested in petting the other horse, General. The owner explained that General was blind in both eyes, the result of an infection that went undetected and untreated when General was abandoned—just like Ariel—many years ago. Upon hearing the sad news, Krischan had one mission and one mission only: To comfort a sweet old horse that needed his love and affection. As Krischan walked toward him, General's ears perked up as he heard Krischan get closer and closer. But General didn't run; rather he stood still and waited for Krischan to get beside him and offer comfort in the form of gentle strokes to the side of his face by a tiny pair of hands belonging to his new and trusted friend.

As I said before, animals just know.

While it may be true that—as Krischan said—Curious George's head was 'bigger than my whole body', it wasn't nearly as big as that little boy's heart.

Just ask the animals.

Animals seem to like me

The important thing is not to stop questioning.
Curiosity has its own reason for existing.
— Albert Einstein

Continuing Education

April 2015

My grandson just spent his weeklong spring break with Cindy and I. After nine days of being G-Pa—that included cameo appearances as chauffeur, cook, playmate and personal assistant -- I learned a thing or two along the way.

Here's what I know now that I didn't know nine days ago:

- When a six-year old asks to play Monkey-in-the-Middle with three adults and volunteers to be the monkey, do not assume the youngster knows the objective of the game is to keep the ball AWAY from them and not throw it directly to them.

- There should never be any crying during a game of Monkey-in-the-Middle. If there is, someone doesn't know the rules. You might want to call the game Keep Away instead of Monkey-in-the-Middle. It could save a whole lot of aggravation… for you and the little ones.

- There are some children who would choose to eat tomatoes on Easter Sunday rather than the speckled robin eggs (malted milk balls) found in their Easter basket. These children may very well be aliens from another planet.

- A six-year old would have you believe a McDonald's Happy Meal covers all four of the major food groups.

- A puppy trumps a McDonald's Happy Meal every time.

- The coolest animal at the zoo is a snake, even though they're not that easy to pet. Apparently 'cool' trumps 'cuddly.'

- Some six-year olds dream of one day having '100 jobs.' After learning that having 100 jobs may be a bit unrealistic, some will settle for being a veterinarian/video game designer.

- There is no limit to how many Teenage Mutant Ninja Turtle cartoons a six-year old can watch in one sitting. Ditto for Scooby Doo cartoons and five-year olds (learned one year ago).

- Six-year olds are perfectly capable of driving a truck. While sitting on the lap of an adult. An adult with both hands on the steering wheel. With one foot on the gas pedal. And the other on the brake. And on a road without another car in sight for miles. Like I said, capable.

- The promise of bubbles and tiny rubber sharks makes the suggestion of a bath a lot more appealing than one offering nothing more than watermelon-scented SpongeBob SquarePants shampoo and body wash.

- There is a cure for everything. It is called chocolate milk and its magical powers simply cannot be denied.

- Six is the age when getting clothing on your birthday is considered 'lame.' Here is a complete list of what isn't considered lame: Toys.

- Rubber dinosaurs can be powerful bargaining chips with six-year old boys.

- Some six-year olds know more about science than most adults can remember, and by 'most' I mean me.

- Six-year olds can find every single toy in a grocery store, even those hidden along the adult hygiene aisle.

I also noticed Krischan still comes up with some of the most profound statements:

- Krischan found a mushroom as we were walking in the woods. He pulled it out of the ground, looked at it and said: 'This mushroom is impressive. I'm taking it home to investigate.'

- Krischan and I were walking deep into the woods. I asked him if he was afraid we wouldn't be able to find our way back out to which he replied: 'No, I put a stick next to a rock and when we come back I'll see it and know where we are.'

- Krischan, Cindy and I were going through his toy chest to see what toys could be passed along to someone younger. Cindy pulled out a foot tall chicken that danced to music when it was turned on. Krischan said 'keep it; it sort of scares me.'

- We also ran across a rubber hockey puck. Cindy: Do you want to keep this? Krischan: What is it? Cindy: It's a hockey puck. Krischan: No, I don't even have a hockey pucker.

One last thing I learned: There's nothing I would have rather done these past nine days than be chauffeur, cook, playmate and personal assistant. They all come with the territory of being a G-Pa, and I wouldn't want it any other way.

Youth has no age.
-Pablo Picasso

Birthday Blues

April 2015

'They grow up way too fast.'

That phrase has never had more meaning than it did a couple weeks ago. It was at Krischan's birthday party. He was turning six, which I found sort of strange because I could have sworn it wasn't that long ago he was still drinking his chocolate milk out of a sippy cup. Certainly it couldn't have been *that* long ago, could it?

Krischan is at an age now where you can see he's still a little boy at heart, but his spoken words indicate his mind is starting to think with the maturity that the kids of my generation didn't realize until they were at least twice his age.

First, the signs of the little boy.

• The party was at a bowling alley/arcade and included several of his friends from school. While it was rather obvious none of them had ever bowled before nor had any idea how, it was also pretty clear that in no way did that take away from their enjoyment of spending the afternoon throwing (notice I didn't say 'rolling') an eight-pound ball towards a pyramid of 10 white objects at the end of the 'runway.' (Note: The bumper guards were in place, thereby ensuring that the ball would knock down at least one pin on their first throw.) Seeing the excitement on all of their faces—they would all stand on the lane and watch as one of them bowled—was a joy to behold. Every time pins were knocked down—one, three, once or twice *all ten*—the excitement shared by the small band of friends came through in random displays of screams, laughter and random bouncing up and down.

- The enthusiasm quickly shifted away from bowling when their party hostess showed up with an apron full of balloons and an air pump. Ladies first: Kaitlyn asked for a pink puppy. Now for the birthday boy: A purple sword. It wasn't long before all of the boys at the party had balloon swords, each one a different color so they would know whose was whose. As if it mattered. Once the swordfight began, Kaitlyn decided she really wanted a sword (goodbye pink pony!) so she could enter the combat. (Kaitlyn, the only girl at the party held her own against the boys.)

- Then came a short—a very, very short time out to enjoy the birthday cake that was covered with blue icing and had an edible shark on top. Everyone caught their breath long enough to watch the birthday boy blow out the flame of a single wax candle in the shape of the number six. Although each child was given a generous slice of cake, it didn't hold their attention for very long because they all had gift cards for the arcade and as I already said by this time they had all caught their breath. *Hello, second wind!* (Note: If it weren't for one particularly hungry G-Pa who *loves* vanilla cake, a whole bunch of cake would have gone to waste. You're welcome.)

- The arcade proved to be the afternoon's main attraction, center of attention and *greatest thing EVER* because for the remaining two hours of the party the energy level of the kids reached the sky. The dark room featuring a maze with red laser beams that had to be avoided at all costs was a huge hit, as evidenced by one pair of youngsters (they entered the maze in pairs) after another exiting the room with beaming smiles on their faces and the same words coming out of their mouths: 'I want to do THAT again!' Eventually the other attractions the arcade had to offer were discovered: The grappling hook that all children today apparently have the inherent ability to master; the life-size two-dimensional Terminator cyborgs that had to be destroyed with life-size laser-firing rifles; and an assortment of old school games (skee ball, air hockey, down-a-clown) that have withstood the test of time and maintained their youthful appeal through the years.

- At the end of the day it was time to trade in all their points (earned at the various games throughout the afternoon) for some prizes. It wasn't long before everyone had their fair share of plastic vampire teeth, super bouncy balls and rubber insects to take home as trophies demonstrating their mastery of the afternoon's challenges.

Now for the signs indicating the boy may not be so little anymore:

- I took Krischan to the men's room and while washing our hands he looked at me and asked: 'G-Pa, you know Kaitlyn? Guess what.' At that moment I had a life-flashing-before-your-eyes moment as to what he was about to say next. 'She's my girlfriend.' 'We held hands.' 'She kissed me.' You can only imagine my relief when he followed with this: 'Her name and my name both start with a K.' The look of relief on my face must have been obvious, judging by the reciprocating look of 'what-did-you-think-I-was-going-to-say' on his.

- After the party we drove to Helen, Georgia where we would be spending the night. At one point during the 90-minute drive my impatience for a fellow driver was displayed in a rash of… well, let's just say 'in a rash.' From the child's seat in the back came this: 'Patience, G-Pa.' I looked back at Krischan, expecting to see a smile on his face and somewhat surprised to discover the stern, parent-like gaze of a little boy well beyond his years in maturity. Make no mistake: He was being dead serious.

It's true what they say about 'out of the mouths of babes…'

The next morning at breakfast Krischan, still obviously tired from the previous day's fun-a-thon looked at me and said in the sincerest voice a six-year old could possibly muster:

'G-Pa, I wish every day was my birthday party.'

It felt good to have my little boy back. After all, he's still got plenty of time to grow up…

The best place to be when you're sad is on Grandpa's lap.
-Author Unknown

Turtle Crossing

April 2015

At the end of my run the other morning I saw a small turtle crossing the one major road in my subdivision; that is to say I think it was crossing but it was hard to tell because he wasn't moving when I found him. I remembered my grandson telling me two days earlier that he had just learned about turtles and tortoises in school. With that in mind I thought it might be a good idea to take the turtle home, show it to Krischan and let him get a feel for what he had learned.

I set the turtle down on the driveway and went inside the house to tell Krischan I had a surprise for him but warning him that is wasn't a toy, video game or Happy Meal. Being the good G-Pa that I am, I didn't want him to have any false hopes or expectations, only to be disappointed because his surprise was merely a reptile--even if it was one that was breathing and ate bugs.

Krischan rushed outside and judging from the look on his face the turtle was a better surprise than anything Mattel, Nintendo or Ronald McDonald had to offer. 'It's a turtle!' he screamed with the excitement of someone who had just stumbled upon the Fountain of Youth.

I told Krischan that when I found the turtle he was wearing a blue mask and therefore must be Michelangelo, the Teenage Mutant Ninja Turtle. He knew instantly I was lying because 'everyone knows Michelangelo wears an orange mask.' Besides, 'Leonardo wears a blue mask and is as big as a human!' Yes sir, you have to wake up pretty early in the morning to pull one over on this kid.

'Did you know turtles live in water and tortoises live on land?' Krischan looked at me waiting for my reply. (Instinctively I knew that *he* knew I had no idea of the distinction between the two. I warned you: You have to wake up pretty early in the morning to pull one over on this kid.)

'No, I didn't,' I replied. 'Where did you learn that?'

'On ABCmouse.com,' he replied. His answer hit me on three levels: (1) He was using the internet for educational purposes. (2) He retained the information and was now relaying it to me. (3) 'Dot-com' rolled off his tongue as easily as 'chicken nuggets' does when he orders a Happy Meal. (*Seriously?* The boy is only six years old!)

We spent the next 30 minutes—or I should say *Krischan* spent the next 30 minutes telling me everything he knew about turtles, nature and why mushroom pizza would be a good idea for dinner later ('because that's what the Teenage Mutant Ninja Turtles eat!'). I smiled pretty much the entire time, appreciating his interest in the subject matter as much as I did his concern for the well-being of his new reptilian friend. Krischan placed several blades of grass and a tray of water in front of ('Let's see, I think I will name him…') Spike.

(I asked him where he got the name 'Spike.' Apparently the Teenage Mutant Ninja Turtles have a pet turtle—*who knew?*—named Spike. Now you know.)

Around lunchtime Cindy took Krischan with her to the grocery store. I was left behind to babysit Spike. (*Spike was in a cardboard box and all I had to do was make sure he didn't climb or jump over the side. Spike was four inches long and the side of the box was eight inches high, so I wasn't too worried. But I did check on him numerous times; just to be safe… and because I don't spend a lot of time on ABCmouse.com and have very little recollection of anything I learned about biology while I was in school and in all sincerity don't really know whether or not a four-inch turtle can climb or jump over an eight-inch wall.*)

When they got back Krischan couldn't wait to tell me the news: He helped a much larger turtle on the same road where I found Spike climb over a curb so it could (presumably) make its way to the lake in our subdivision. He showed me with his hands (held about 12 inches apart) how big the turtle was and said it was Spike's mother. I asked him how he knew and he said 'I just do.' I didn't argue with him because as you may recall I know virtually nothing about biology.

After an afternoon of holding Spike, watching Spike crawl and making sure Spike didn't get lodged behind the freezer in the garage, we turned our attention to deciding what would be in Spike's best interest in the long run. I told Krischan turtles enjoyed being around water and since there was a creek running alongside and behind our house it would be the perfect place to take him. (If any of that is true, then consider it a lucky guess; I know nothing about biology. Don't make me tell you again.).

We walked down the hill to the creek. Krischan set Spike down on the bank, about two inches from the water. Spike hit the creek with a splash and immediately started paddling upstream (the creek originates from the lake, about one half-mile upstream from our house). Krischan said Spike was going home to see his mom at the exact moment Spike climbed onto the bank on the opposite side of the stream. Suddenly Krischan had a change of heart: 'Go get Spike, G-Pa.'

Just about that time Spike jumped back in the water and started swimming downstream. Krischan followed the turtle, running along the bank all the way up to where the creek funnels through a tunnel and continues on the other side. Alas, the bank ended at the tunnel and at least for the time being Krischan had seen the last of Spike.

I could see the sadness in Krischan's face. I tried my best to ease the pain. 'Don't worry; we'll see Spike again someday. He'll be happy out here and I'm guessing his mom will be joining him here very soon.'

I walked back towards the house and after 20 paces or so I noticed Krischan wasn't right behind me like he normally is when we take walks behind the house. Instead he was standing in the exact same spot I had left him, still as a statue. I called his name several times, each time louder than the next. He didn't budge, even after my tone had a hint of anger in it after a minute or so of calling to him. I walked back over to Krischan and was about to grab his arm when I noticed the front of his shirt was soaking wet… from the tears he had been shedding since I walked away a couple of minutes earlier. 'I miss my friend,' he sobbed. His lips were quivering, his eyes were red and his nose was dripping almost as much as his eyes. 'I'll never see my friend again.'

I was at a loss for words. Almost, that is.

I reminded Krischan of the turtles' role in nature (in my best ABCmouse.com voice) and how much happier Spike would be living in the creek behind our house: Spike's Creek, we'd call it. Krischan listened as I spoke, but clearly he wasn't convinced as the tears continued to pour. 'You should feel good because Spike knows what you did for him was a good thing and for that he will always be your friend.' Closer but still no cigar, although the tears were now slowing to a trickle. 'You will always be in his heart and he'll always be your friend. Always.' At last; no more tears. One more glance at Spike's Creek and we walked back to the house, hand-in-hand.

When Krischan's mother came to pick him up later that day he couldn't wait to tell her about Spike. I couldn't hear everything he told her, but I did notice his eyes were wide as saucers, he had a smile on his face the entire time and the last thing he said was something about Spike living in the creek behind the house.

I may not know anything about biology, but I do know a little something about grandsons.

Set your goals high, and don't stop until you get there.
– Bo Jackson

100,000 Miles

May 2015

Sometimes stories just write themselves. This is one such story.

It was the first Saturday in May. The weather couldn't have been more perfect: Sunny, gentle breeze and temperatures hovering around 70 degrees. Forty or so runners had gathered at the beautiful Bear Creek Farm in Moreland, Georgia to run for eight hours around a 1.02-mile asphalt loop amongst the residents, most notably the magnificent horses who were more than willing to run side-by-side with the runners.

This was the 13th year of the event and the first time I was able to run in it because it was also the first time it was being directed by someone other then myself. I was on my 23rd loop when Cindy, her friend Jan and my grandson Krischan arrived to partake of the festivities. Krischan's first comment to me when I finished #23: 'What took you so long, G-Pa?' He couldn't have been waiting for me for more than seven or eight minutes.

I asked him if he wanted to run a loop with me. I'm not sure I had the entire question out of my mouth before he was taking off—intuitively, I might add—on the loop in the correct direction: Counterclockwise, just as he was taught several years ago when I took him to the local high school track for the first time.

As he is prone to do, Krischan took off like a jackrabbit. More accurately, like a hare… as in the story of the tortoise and the hare. We talked about that fable a week ago and Cindy and I tried to convey the moral of the story: Slow but steady wins the race. I caught up to him and reminded him of it. He slowed down—if only for a couple of seconds before speeding off. This cycle repeated for the entire loop and the next.

As we approached the gazebo (the start/finish line of each loop) I pulled slightly ahead and told him he was the hare and I was the tortoise. His reply: 'No, this is the story of the Krischan and the G-Pa' before taking the lead and keeping it the remaining 150 yards back to the gazebo. So much for Aesop and his fables.

Krischan stopped at the gazebo to get a drink and some snacks, courtesy of the other runners in the event. In no particular order he dined on Gummi bears, Doritos, cookies, M & M's, Pringles potato chips and cupcakes and drank (also in no particular order) Gatorade, Coke, water and Sprite. I ran the next loop alone and when I returned to the gazebo Krischan was gone: He was doing a couple more loops with Cindy and Jan. Krischan would join me again on my 30th loop (I would run 31 when all was said and done) and provided the most entertaining 15 minutes I can remember.

Here's what Krischan had in store for me (as well as the other runners on the course):
Runner: How far have you run?
Krischan: Eight hours (he knew it was an eight-hour run, thus the reference), but it doesn't feel like eight hours.

Runner: How did you become such an awesome runner?

Krischan: That's because I work out.

As we approached a runner who had told me she wanted to meet Krischan:
Me: *This lady up ahead wants to meet you.*
Krischan: *Why? Is she a fan of mine?*

Random comment by Krischan to me: *Did you know red blood cells carry oxygen to your body?*
Random comment by Krischan to another runner: *Too much running is bad for you.* (You can blame this one on me: Krischan has seen me after some of my longer runs.)

Random comment by Krischan to a runner drinking a beer in the gazebo after we finished the loop: *Too much beer is bad for you.* (Again, my fault.)

Random comment to a line of four men taking a walk break on the course (keep in mind they had been out on the course for over six hours at the time): *Come on, you slowpokes. You all need to stop walking and talking. Let's run!* (This followed by another burst of hare-like speed, of course.)

Krischan sat at a picnic table beneath the gazebo as I finished my final loop, at which point I took a seat in a canvas chair and began counting loops as the runners still on the course went by. Krischan grabbed a canvas chair, plopped it down next to me and before he sat down ran out on the course to run another loop with someone he had never met. Six-year olds know no strangers, you know.

About 15 minutes later Krischan came running up the hill towards the gazebo, albeit with a different runner than the one he had joined at the beginning of the loop. He took a seat in the chair next to me, sat for a good—oh, 25 seconds or so and joined another runner he had never met to run yet another loop. Fifteen minutes later he returned, again with a runner other than the one he left with. The runner commented when she ran by: 'Your grandson sure kept me entertained.'

When all was said and done, Krischan had completed nine of the 1.02-mile loops; nine very, very hilly loops all within a time frame that couldn't have been much more than two hours. Before today the most he had ever run was one mile. As he took a seat in the canvas chair next to me one last time he looked over at the grease board listing the top three males and females and asked why his name wasn't listed. I went over and wrote his name at the bottom of the board with a '9' next to it. He promptly ran over and changed it to 59, later changing it to 100,000. I asked him how on earth he managed to run that far. 'I started early.' That boy has an answer for everything.

After the awards ceremony and some post-race conversation and refreshments it was time to clean up the gazebo and surrounding area. Krischan was a real trooper, putting plastic cups in the trash can and making sure everyone got some of the Doritos from the bag he was guarding with his life. On the way home—a 20-minute drive at most, Krischan was out like a light.

That's what happens when you're only six years old and just ran 100,000 miles.

Teaching children about the natural world should be treated as one of the most important events in their lives.
— Thomas Berry

Nature Boy

May 2015

Wooooo!!!

People everywhere recognize the battle cry of Ric Flair, the self-proclaimed 'Nature Boy' of professional wrestling. For decades Flair's stature amongst the best having competed in the 'squared circle'—as wrestling rings are known in the business--is undeniable. His ability to attract both interest in his sport and fans to arenas around the world has been firmly established. His right to the nickname 'Nature Boy' has never been questioned.

Until now, that is.

Move over, Ric Flair. There's a new Nature Boy in town, and his name is Krischan.

Krischan's interest in nature started at an early age. When he was too young to walk Cindy and I took him for rides in his stroller to a nearby lake. Once we stumbled upon a family of ducks along the shore or an array of turtles sunning on an old log, Krischan would sit back and take it all in for as long as Cindy and I were willing to let him.

When Krischan was old enough to walk he wanted me to take him to feed the horses. It didn't matter *which* horses, he just wanted to FEED THE HORSES. Quick trips to the grocery store for apples and carrots were standard operating procedure for a couple of years, as were the subsequent trips to any of a multitude of farms and pastures populated by equines of all colors, shapes and sizes. It was a joy watching the excitement on Krischan's face as the horses lined up at the fence to share in whatever their little three and later four year old friend would pull out of his grocery back next.

Long walks with Krischan have always been an adventure. Now that he's near the end of kindergarten, it always amazes me to hear what he has to say as we traverse the great outdoors:

'Rain is nature's friend; it feeds the flowers.'

'The sun keeps the planet warm. The animals, too.'

'The stars in the sky tell you where you are.'

'Reptiles are our friends because they eat insects.'

The hits just keep on coming.

When I'm with Krischan he always manages to keep my attention. After all, I've been out of school for a good many years and it's always interesting to find out how much Krischan knows... as well as how much I've forgotten (a lot, apparently).

I've never seen anyone who can entertain himself as much simply by being in the great outdoors. It could be in the front yard... in the back yard... in the woods behind the house... at the lake up the street. It matters not: If it's outdoors, there's an adventure waiting to be discovered by a certain wide-eyed, eager to experience and learn six-year old boy willing to take it all in.

Krischan's appreciation for nature really shined through last Saturday as he was running in a one-mile fun run on an asphalt path that meandered through a multitude of grassy fields. We were running together and Krischan was on pace to run a personal best time when he abruptly stopped in his tracks. He bent over and spent a good 30 seconds or more rescuing an earthworm that had found its way into the middle of the asphalt path. He picked it up and calmly returned it to its natural habitat, the dirt on one side of the asphalt. When we resumed running he told me he feared the worm would be crushed by the runners and wanted to save it because 'worms are good for nature.'

Although Krischan missed beating his personal best time by a mere 10 seconds, it was clear to me that the boy definitely has his priorities in order.

Move over, Ric Flair. There's a new Nature Boy in town.

Wooooo!!!

I love nature!

One touch of nature makes the whole world kin.
-William Shakespeare

I'm your Captain

June 2015

'I don't want to go to the river. I want to stay HERE!'

Try asking a six-year old to leave a water park on a hot summer day and you're likely to get the same reaction.

The 'here' Krischan is referring to is a water park in Helen, Georgia. Krischan was there with me, Cindy and his Uncle Josh. What does the water park have to offer? Here's what the website has to say:

The 1,000' Lazy River

When the river (the Chattahoochee) *is low, the Water Park is the place to be: We have four large waterslides and a 1000' lazy river with controlled water, which means you don't get stuck ever!*
NO ROCKS, NO WALKING, NO SNAKES, NO WORRIES!

We hit the water slides first. One is nothing more than a gigantic sliding board with a couple of humps that you ride on a bath tub mat with your feet facing forward while either sitting up or lying on your back. Krischan's first attempt was nothing short of a disaster: Somehow his body was entirely turned around by the time he crash landed in the pool at the end of the slide. But that didn't stop him from wanting to do it again. On his third attempt he sat on his mat perfectly still and perfectly straight (think of Aladdin riding on his magic carpet) and had his sights firmly set on bigger game.

In this case the bigger game was the other water slide. Starting from the same elevation as the first slide, this one followed a serpentine path through a long, dark tunnel. Either one or two people were allowed at one time, so long as a rubber raft was used. Krischan wanted to ride with me and insisted I ride in the front. I must say he made a wise choice. My legs were hanging out over the front of the raft and as we took one 90-degree hairpin turn after another at 60 miles an hour I just knew it was only a matter of time before one of my legs snapped like a twig when it slammed into one of the corners. I can't tell you how relieved I was when we splash-landed into the pool and both of my legs were still intact. Then I looked over at Krischan to find an expression on his face that I'm pretty sure was the same one I had on mine.

Now it was time for the 1,000-foot Lazy River. Imagine a large oval-shaped moat with an ever-so-slight current. Now hop on a rubber tube, lie back and let the current do the work. Or if your name happens to be Krischan you could always hop OFF the rubber tube, run with the current in two-foot-six-inch deep water that up to your neck and try your best to elude your G-Pa who is chasing after you because he doesn't want to lose you in a sea of pink polyurethane.

'Enough of this,' I thought to myself. *'More, more, more!'* Krischan screamed at the top of his lungs.

Fortunately I had two allies who shared my thoughts. *'It's time for us to tube down the river,'* Cindy announced.

'I don't want to go to the river. I want to stay HERE!'

'You'll love the river. There are trees and rocks and fish and mountains and lots of nature and you know how much you love nature,' I added.

'But I like it right here!'

'You'll like tubing on the river more.' With Josh chiming in it's now three against one.

'I'm going on the slide. Again.'

'No you're not. We're all getting on the bus that's going to take us to the river and we're doing it NOW.' Cindy had to resort to playing the trump card that comes with being the grandmother. Krischan walked to the bus stop with slumped shoulders and a pooched-out lower lip; he had no idea he was only minutes away from a two-hour ride down the Chattahoochee River that he would later refer to as *'the best day ever!'*

After a 10-minute bus ride we were two miles upstream where we were issued our rubber tubes and began our ride down the river. We had the option of tethering two tubes together, so Krischan immediately called 'dibs' on his G-Pa. Seconds later I was knee-deep in the river (Krischan was waist-deep) and climbing inside my tube as Krischan was doing a swan dive into his. We were barely on our way downstream before Krischan announced to anyone within earshot that he was 'the captain.' It didn't take a rocket scientist to figure out who was going to be his first mate.

For the next two hours I have to admit that Krischan and I had the time of our lives. By the time we got to the end of our journey we had become quite adept at navigating our way around protruding rocks, beneath overhanging branches and through other tubers at complete standstills for one reason or another. I also discovered the hard way what my duties were as first mate:

- Make sure the tubes of the captain and the first mate remain tethered together, even if the captain is responsible for untethering them because he finds it amusing.

- Skim the bottom of the river for rocks of appropriate size and weight for the captain to throw (for his amusement) in the vicinity of the first mate's tube.

- Do whatever is necessary to avoid protruding rocks, overhanging branches and other tubers at complete standstills. This will at times require the strength of an ox, the flexibility of an Olympic gymnast and the hypervigilance of a fighter pilot.

- Answer to the demands of the captain at all times.

As for the duties of the captain, from what I observed here is the complete list:

- Constantly announce to anyone within earshot that he is the captain.

At the end of the day we all went out for dinner at a local restaurant. More than once Krischan referred to the day's events as 'the best day ever.'

As for me, after paddling furiously with both arms for most of the afternoon to ensure our tubes kept moving down the river and staying out of harm's way, all I could think about was an old joke that was really hitting home:

I just flew in from California and boy are my arms tired.

Running isn't a sport for pretty boys...
It's about the sweat in your hair and the blisters on your feet.
-Paul Maurer

On the Right Track

June 2015

'I've been here before.'

Those were the first words out of Krischan's mouth when we stepped onto the 400-meter track at Riley Field to participate in the Summer Track Classic, a series of track meets held on Wednesday nights open to runners of all ages and abilities.

'But there weren't this many people here last time.'

It had been a while since the two of us had been to Riley Field. Slightly over three years, in fact. But Krischan remembered it as if it was yesterday, and apparently those memories were good ones because he couldn't wait to get out on the track and 'run like before' *(his words, although that last word may have actually been 'afore'—I'll get to work on that).*

The first event of the evening was the 800-meter run. There were three heats and the runners were divided up according to their projected finishing time. The fastest runners ran the first heat. Krischan, a head shorter and a decade younger than everyone else ran in the third heat. I offered to run with him—primarily to keep him from starting out too fast as he is prone to do when he runs alone—but said I'd be OK standing at the finish line taking photos.

Although I was a bit surprised when he said he'd run alone, I was more than happy to step aside and capture the moment in pictures.

As Krischan was standing behind the starting line I noticed he had his hands on his hips and was swaying from side to side, similar to what he sees me doing when I'm doing practicing yoga (perhaps 'attempting' is a better word). Apparently he was listening the many times I told him 'yoga is good for you' over the past two years. Apparently he *wasn't* listening, however when I reminded him *two minutes earlier* to start out slow and finish strong.

After the starter's pistol was fired, Krischan took off like a rocket. Initially he was running neck-and-neck amongst the leaders, his tiny head bobbing up and down and belly-high to everyone else. He was holding his own against runners with strides nearly twice as long as his... for about 200 meters before slowing down to a walk that lasted... until he saw me I was standing by the time clock) and started running even faster than he had been in the beginning. The burst of speed lasted until he rounded the corner at the beginning of his second lap... and once again slowed down to a walk.

Exactly five-and-a-half minutes after he answered the call of his first starter's pistol, Krischan finished his first initial 800-meter run.

Next Krischan ran the 50-meter dash with seven other six-and-seven-year olds. While I didn't notice his finishing time, I did get a killer photo of him crossing the finish line: The picture paints a thousand words, if I do say so myself.

The mile was next: Four complete laps—and then some—around the 400-meter track. Krischan had run quite a few one-mile fun runs on Saturday mornings with other boys and girls around his age, but this was the first time he would be running with adults and members of the local high school cross country team. This time he wanted me to run with him so I could, as he put it 'keep me from running too fast; you know, like the Flash.'

We started the first lap at a conservative pace and as we rounded the first corner—about 100 meters into the race Krischan first looked back over his shoulder, then looked at me and said 'Where are all the people behind us?' 'Krischan,' I said, 'There *isn't* anyone behind us.' We ended up running—and walking a couple times when Krischan said it felt like someone was pinching his stomach (a side stitch, no doubt) just two laps before we called it a night.

Now that I've had time to think about Krischan's first track workout I've identified a couple of things besides the word 'afore' to work on, such as:

- Making sure Krischan understands he is not the only one using the track. Several times he wandered out on the track while others were running. Watching him dodging other runners—and watching other runners dodge him reminded me of a life-size game of Whack-A-Mole played out on a large rubber mat. Fortunately, perhaps miraculously the particular mole I was watching never got whacked.

- Making sure Krischan understands that certain events (50-meter, 100-meter and 200-meter) require the runner to stay in their assigned lane. Watching him in those events reminded me of a miniature game of running shoe-wearing bumper cars.

- Making sure Krischan understands it is not proper etiquette when another runner comes up from behind him to run as hard as he possibly can in an attempt to avoid the inevitable moment when he is lapped.

To summarize: Krischan had a blast, but it's definitely a work in progress.

On the drive home I noticed Krischan's face was red as a beet and his shirt and hair were soaked with perspiration. He rolled down his window and leaned his head out so he could feel the wind blowing into his face. I doubt there was anyone on the planet without four legs and a tail that could possibly have enjoyed that simple, wonderful moment more.

As we pulled into the driveway Krischan rolled up his window. I noticed he was touching his hair on various spots on his head. 'G-Pa, my sweat is all gone!' The level of excitement in his voice was more appropriate for telling me he had just spotted a real live unicorn. 'Now I don't have to take a bath.'

I explained that the sweat was now dry and he would still need a bath. If you could have seen the look on his face you would have thought I had just told him I ran over the unicorn with my car.

After his bath and a quick dinner it wasn't long before he was ready for bed. As I tucked him in I asked him if he enjoyed his first track meet. He said he did and just before nodding off asked me if I would wake him up in the morning so he could run with me. I said I would but in my mind I knew I had no intention of waking up a six-year old boy after only five hours of sleep.

The boy needs his sleep at that age. Without it there's a good chance his G-Pa just might lap him, and I know Krischan wouldn't be happy about that.

Learning is a treasure that will follow its owner everywhere.
– Chinese Proverb

The Graduate

June 2015

Since he first learned to talk, Krischan has asked me virtually every question a grandson could possibly ask a grandfather. To name a few:

What happens when the tooth fairy's tooth falls out?
If the moon is made of green cheese, then why is it yellow?
Why do you shave your face and Yia-Yia shaves her legs?
How do babies come out of their mommy's tummy? Are they pooped out?

I thought I'd heard most everything until this one came out of his mouth last Friday night:

G-Pa, are you proud of me?

Here's some background to give the question a little perspective: Twelve hours earlier Krischan graduated from kindergarten. He couldn't wait to tell me he was now 'a first grader.' He was obviously bursting with pride and wanted to know if the feeling was mutual.

Wow, my grandson is going into the first grade. It seems like only yesterday I was spoon-feeding him his pureed fruits and vegetables... teaching him not call his toys 'mine' when playing with others... reading him *The Cat in the Hat.*

Over the nine months Krischan has been keeping me well informed of what he's been learning in kindergarten. I remember my mom and dad asking me what I learned in school when I was a young boy and my answer was always the same: 'Nothing.' Krischan is different; he always has something new to tell me at the end of the week.

I learned to count to 100. One, two, three…*
(*Yes, he made it all the way to 100)

Blue and yellow make green.

George Washington was our first President; he's the Father of our Country.

Frogs are tadpoles before they become frogs.

A paleontologist is someone who studies dinosaurs.

But wait, it gets better. The past five or six weeks Krischan has been doing simple arithmetic—adding and subtracting single-digit numbers, primarily—in his head. For the really tough ones he may break out a finger or two but for the most part, as I said, he does it all in his head.

He's also starting to read. The first time I realized it was when we were at the Golden Arches a few weeks ago and he started reading the side of his Happy Meal box to me. I listened intently as he sounded aloud one letter after another, finally saying them all together until he could come up with a word he recognized. I know it's been a while but I don't think I was that far along until third or fourth grade (forgive me; as I said it's been a while).

With a huge smile on his face Krischan proudly showed me his green Kindergarten Keepsake notebook chronicling his first year in the public education system. Inside the flap of the front cover was a Certificate for his Excellence in Social Studies. According to his mom he was the only child in kindergarten to receive this distinction. I asked Krischan what social studies were and his reply was honest, sincere and concise: 'I don't know.' While he understands most of our National Holidays, the duties of the President and the words to the Pledge of Allegiance, Krischan doesn't recognize these things as social studies; he knows them as 'America.'

As I mentioned previously last Friday night Krischan was anxious to know if I was proud of his promotion to the first grade. Knowing he wanted to hear the words from his G-Pa out loud I answered: 'Yes I am very, *very* proud of you.'

If Krischan hadn't been so excited and paid closer attention he might have noticed a tear or two welling up in my eyes.

If he had I wouldn't have needed to say a word. The answer would have been obvious.

Even to a first grader.

G-Pa says it's not too early to apply

Autumn is really the best of the seasons;
and I'm not sure that old age isn't the best part of life.
-C.S. Lewis

Losing My Marbles

July 2015

I knew the day would come. I just didn't know it would be this soon.

Or that it would hit me with both barrels.

The day I'm referring to is the day I realized I was starting to lose my marbles.

Allow me to give you both barrels so you can judge for yourself.

Barrel One: I spent the better part of 10 minutes looking around the house for the keys to my car. I finally found them… snugly in the palm of my right hand where they had been for the entire time I spent looking for them. While only the tip of the iceberg, there have been enough incidents such as this one that have in no uncertain terms highlighted the fact that I'm losing it, whatever 'it' may be… or more accurately, used to be.

Barrel Two: My grandson has discovered my marble collection in the two-gallon glass aquarium in the guest bedroom. He considers the marbles to be his, seeing as he occasionally sleeps in the guest bedroom, has some of his clothes in the dresser in the guest bedroom and the majority of his toy dinosaurs reside in the guest bedroom. Ergo, the marbles are his.

Back to Barrel One: I've sensed this coming for the past several years; this slow-but-ever-so-sure deterioration of what used to be a pretty keen mind. It seemed like only yesterday I was able to tell whether or not I had a set of keys in my hand. Boy has that ship sailed. Now I can't remember names, have trouble driving after dark and it takes me 10 minutes longer than it used to getting ready for work in the morning.

Back to Barrel Two: I've taught Krischan how to play marbles… the old fashioned way. You may remember: Pick a shooter (preferably one of the larger marbles) for yourself, put the rest of the marbles inside of an imaginary circle (a better option is to play in the dirt and draw a circle in the dirt with a stick) and take turns shooting at the marbles by flicking your shooter with your thumb and claiming any marbles that are 'hit.' Is Krischan any good? Let's just say where there's a will there's a way: If he decides he wants to hit a particular marble, one way or another it's going to happen. For example he may call for a 'do-over' if one of his flicks doesn't hit a marble, drop his shooter directly on top of his intended target or simply tell me he hit a particular marble when the truth of the matter is he missed it by at least a foot or more.

My marble collection has been with me for many, many years. To say that it is one of my pride and joys would not be far from the truth. In that aquarium are marbles that once upon a time belonged to Pappy, my mother's father; Robert and Don, my wife's two older brothers; and a lot of my friends because I won them playing 'keepsies' when I was Krischan's age.

I had names for some of the marbles: Steelies (made completely of steel), puries (you can see completely through them), boulders (the oversized ones that Krischan likes to shoot with), cat eyes (if you saw one you'd know why) and some really old marbles made of wood I never knew what to call.

I guess you could say my marble collection is very near and dear to me. They represent several generations of family, a multitude of memories and how simple it was many, many years ago to have fun.

Once more for Barrel One: I'm going to hold onto whatever I've got left for as long as I possibly can.

Once more for Barrel Two: One day Krischan will own my treasured marble collection. I can't think of anyone I'd rather have it after I'm gone. These marbles I won't mind losing.

However, I can't say the same for the ones over in Barrel One.

Epilogue

I've got to be honest. Earlier I mentioned writing this book for Krischan.

I'll admit: I also wrote this book for me.

As I grow older I want to be able to occasionally read a chapter or two and reminisce about the magical times when Krischan was young and I was going through the first few years of being a G-Pa. This book will allow me to savor all of these wonderful memories for a lifetime.

Besides, as Krischan so appropriately said to me a few weeks before his sixth birthday:

G-Pa, as you get older your remembery won't be as good as it used to be.

The kid knows.

I wouldn't change our relationship for anything in this world. It's hard to put into words, but the exchange in the next paragraph pretty much sums it up:

I was sitting between Krischan and Cindy on the couch and the three of us were watching a movie. Krischan had a bag of candy in his hand and extended his arm in front of me so that the candy was actually closer to Cindy than me. Krischan asked 'do you want some candy?' Cindy replied 'no thank you' to which Krischan came back with:

'I was talking to G-Pa.'

Acknowledgements

The cover art was provided by Krischan from a drawing he did a couple of months after his 5th birthday. He wasn't trying to imitate the works of Henri Matisse; any resemblance is merely a coincidence.

The photographs are from the personal collection of G-Pa, who considers them among his favorites from the thousands of pictures he took of Krischan in the first 76 months of his life. *(You're very welcome, Target photo lab!)*

My heartfelt appreciation to Susanne Thurman--a grandmother of 10--for her help getting these photographs in this book.

A special thank you to everyone who has touched and/or made an impression on Krischan's life.

Finally, for all of the grandparents who 'get it,' please know that writing this book has been my pleasure. I hope you enjoyed it, and more importantly I hope you have a similar relationship with your grandchild or grandchildren. It's something pretty special, isn't it?

Printed in the United States
By Bookmasters